The people of Kosovo – both the cle: agogically exploited Serbs – now k humanitarian friends were. One of tl and parliamentary advocates has been ~~D~~. ~~Denis~~ MacShane. This will surprise none who know of his record on human rights. The book will stand as a monument to a harsh time and to the fortitude that overcame it.

Christopher Hitchens

Denis MacShane knows the Balkans well, and his book is full of insights on the region. He reminds us why the Balkans matter and why the EU must not stint in its efforts to encourage reconciliation between Serbs and Kosovars.

Charles Grant – Centre for European Reform

In this passionate advocacy for full recognition of Kosovo, MacShane does history of the present like nobody else. He has lived it and contributed to making it, and recounts it with his famous mix of laser sharp analysis, historical scholarship, eloquent advocacy and wry humour which has earned him many friends in the region and in the rest of Europe. A must-read on the fascinating and tragic story of southeast Europe and for all those in Belgrade who understand that true reconciliation between Serbia and Kosovo remains the key to unlocking Serbia's European future.

Kalypso Nicolaïdis, Professor of International Relations,
University of Oxford

Denis MacShane is the best-known Europe Minister Britain has had but, more than that, he is a creative and provocative thinker. This book is a lively and readable study of the Serbia-Kosovo imbroglio, which will be of interest to experts and lay-readers alike.

Mark Leonard, Director, European Council for Foreign Relations

Kosovo needs true friends, like Denis MacShane. Passion powers his pen; and this succinct account of past traumas and present choices is enlivened by a sympathetic understanding drawn from first hand experience, as minister, emissary and friend.

Lord Kerr of Kinlochard, Permanent Under Secretary, Foreign and
Commonwealth Office, Head of Diplomatic Service 1997–2002

The agony of Kosovo could not be balanced by the joy that was to be derived from it...the agony of Kosovo must have been purely itself, pain upon pain, newly born in acuteness for each generation, throughout five centuries.

Rebecca West, *Black Lamb and Grey Falcon*

WHY KOSOVO STILL MATTERS

Rt Hon Dr Denis MacShane MP

First published in Great Britain in 2011 by
Haus Publishing Ltd
70 Cadogan Place
London SW1X 9AH
www.hauspublishing.com

A CIP catalogue record for this book is available from the British Library

ISBN 978-1-907822-39-1

Typeset in Minion by MacGuru Ltd
Printed in the United Kingdom

Contents

Foreword

I had little idea when more than forty years ago I first travelled through the Balkans that this region would become
part of my political life. There are too many friends with whom
I have discussed the region to list here. As a Foreign Office
minister I have been privileged to meet many of the leaders
of nations and communities in the region. My friend Alex
Rondos, Ambassador Extraordinary in Greece, has been a
constant inspiration. I wonder what happened to the 10-point
peace plan for the Balkans we drew up at his hillside house in
Hydra in 2005.

Senior officials at the Foreign and Commonwealth Office
were wise and travelling with them as we waited in the airports of Europe to get to Pristina, Belgrade, Zagreb, Skopje and
Sarajevo allowed time for intense discussion with some of the
most knowledgeable experts and public servants Britain has.
Her Majesty's Ambassadors in the Balkans were always friendly
and helpful. It was an all-male tribe when I first went there as a
minister. It is good to see women diplomats now being properly
promoted.

I don't think there is any political difference on what needs
to be done in the Balkans and I wish Foreign Secretary William
Hague and his team well. I hope that my friend, Kathy Ashton,
the EU's High Representative for Foreign Policy and her chief
Balkans adviser, the learned British diplomat, Robert Cooper,
all good luck as they seek to achieve what escaped me and

British ministers in the first decade of the 21st century, namely a final lasting peace in the Balkans.

Misha Glenny is one of our great writers on Balkans politics and history. I first accompanied Misha in his petrol-stinking Audi, on a foray somewhere in the region when it was necessary to fill up his car. The supply of fuel was so unreliable at the time that we had to transport large containers. We bumped around in what seemed to be a mobile bomb.

Over many years, conversations with numerous journalists, notably the *Guardian*'s Ian Traynor, and Daniel Korski of the European Council of Foreign Relations, have provided invaluable insights. London has the world's best foreign policy institutions and I have had the privilege of serving for a number of years on the Council of the Royal Institute of International Affairs. Its Chatham House meetings are worth more than the subscription as are the excellent International Affairs and World Today.

I lived and worked in Switzerland, France and Germany before becoming an MP so reading their newspapers has been useful in taking perspectives beyond the Anglosphere press.

I am grateful to the House of Commons Library for the efficiency of the staff in producing books and reports on demand. I cannot begin to list the politicians, activists, academics, writers and witnesses I have discussed Kosovo with in innumerable seminars and conferences, especially fellow delegates on the Council of Europe.

I have served as a UK delegate to the parliamentary assemblies of the Council of Europe and NATO. Both have produced reports and discussed Kosovo. At the former I listened to thoughtful Serb laments and protests, as well as more boiler-plate interventions by Russian delegates. Even if I disagree, listening to the other point of view has been useful.

My friend Avdul Gula has been a tireless advocate of Kosovo and has both travelled there with me and subsequently kept me in touch with what is happening in his country while building a family and business in London. Lea Renoux and Muriel Kahane helped with preparing the text. Barbara Schwepcke is a wonderful publisher.

I would like to dedicate this book to a friend who for more than forty years has made me think and laugh about international politics more than anyone else. Christopher Hitchens is beyond price as a comrade, companion and co-conspirator in the pursuit of freedom and fairness.

Denis MacShane, London, Pristina, Rotherham, July 2011

1

Mil-Who? Kos-Where?

The scene is a gathering of the world's powerful union leaders in Montreal in June 1988. Speaking to them was an important European political figure. Now forgotten except to students of the history of Germany's Social Democratic Party, Peter Glotz was then the party's general secretary. He was a Bavarian intellectual, a close friend of Willy Brandt and Helmut Schmidt. He had been one of the brains behind the revival of West German social democracy. Like all German political intellectuals he spoke good English and had travelled across the Atlantic to talk to what he thought was an important gathering.

The world seemed firmly under the control of conservatives like Ronald Reagan, Margaret Thatcher and Helmut Kohl. As he switched from criticizing their economic and social policies Glotz's voice rose in passion. "I believe we are seeing in Europe today the rise of a new fascism, a terrible, horrible nationalism that will plunge Europe back into the dark ages of conflict and war. In Kosovo the Serb leader, Slobodan Milošević has made a speech, the likes of which I thought would never be heard again in Europe. Unless he is stopped there will be a terrible conflict in the Balkans."

The sleepy trade union leaders from Europe, America, Canada, Japan, South Africa, Korea, India and overseas representatives of the banned Solidarity trade union movement in Poland just let the words roll over them. I prided myself on some knowledge of the politics of Europe. But I had no idea what Peter Glotz was talking about. Mil – who? Kos – where? Who was this man Glotz said threatened the peace of the world? Where was this place he was talking about?

I had hitchhiked from Munich to Athens as a student, sleeping rough in the different towns and villages as I made my way down through the great cities of the Western Balkans before arriving in Thessaloniki and then on to Athens to link up with other friends from the Oxford University Drama Society where we were to stage a performance of 'Agamemnon' at the theatre in Delphi.

I had taken other trips to different cities in what my generation had always called Yugoslavia. I had holidayed in Dubrovnik. But Kosovo? In 1988, I knew nothing of its history, I could not have placed the 2-million strong nation on the map of Europe. I was not alone. In the tenth edition of Encyclopaedia Britannica published in 1902 there is no entry for Kosovo. Fast forward eighty years to the *Meyers Taschen-Lexikon Geschichte*, a six-volume historical dictionary published in Germany in 1982, and there is still no entry for Kosovo.

In 1997, ten years after Milošević's speech in Kosovo fired the starting pistol of the Balkan wars, I was working in the Foreign Office as an MP and political aide to the Foreign Secretary, Robin Cook. By then, of course, we knew where Kosovo was. We knew who Milošević was. But even then there was little expertise. At one meeting with the then Minister for Europe, Keith Vaz, he listened with a benign smile on his face as officials explained the importance of dealing with the Kosovo question. After a bit he looked up and said: "Can somebody just draw me a little map and show me where Kosovo is?" It was a fair question.

This short book will attempt to explain where Kosovo is and why it is important that, more than a decade after the end of the war that freed its people from torture, terror and tyranny, the Kosovans and their nation state should be allowed to go forward as part of the community of European nations. It is written to explain to a new generation of politicians in my own country, some of whom were still students when the terrible decade of the Balkan wars erupted, why everyone who cares for the peace and prosperity of Europe should support the just and necessary ambitions of the people of Kosovo to be allowed along with Serbs and Croatians and Slovenes and Bosnians and Macedonians to be granted the right to live as a nation with its own state.

Sadly, international politics still seeks to prevent this happening. In the global chess game called Power Politics Kosovo is still used as a pawn on the international chequered board of rivalry between major world powers. So while 80 of the 192 UN members recognize Kosovan independence, declared on 17 February 2008, Serbia continues to regard Kosovo as the Autonomous Province Kosovo and Metochia, and so part of its territory. Many people in Serbia understandably feel that they have been victims in the last twenty years of a giant international swindle as the once powerful federal nation they dominated collapsed into competing rival mini-states leaving them with a bitter past and without a friendly future. Hanging on to an idea that Kosovo belongs to them is a similar reflex that makes some Germans nostalgic for the pre-1939 Reich cry of "*Schlesien bleibt unser!*" (Silesia belongs to us).

But Belgrade too also allows itself too easily to be used as a pawn by Russia and the Kremlin power-holders who believe in a zero-sum game of world politics. What we have we hold. What we can stop happening we will stop happening. We will not come to any agreement with our rivals (even if we now call them partners) unless we get an equal or better concession from them. The people of Kosovo and the people of Serbia are both victims of this subtracted value vision of world politics.

*Kosovo lies at the heart of the Western Balkans, only one of the seven
nations that emerged after the break-up of Yugoslavia.*

This narrative and argument is based on more than a decade's engagement in Kosovo. I entered the Commons in 1994 at the height of British Conservative appeasement of the man and the regime that Peter Glotz had rightly raised the cry of alarm about in 1988. I then worked in the Foreign Office with Robin Cook and closely with Jonathan Powell, a former diplomat who was Tony Blair's Chief of Staff as the Kosovan crisis rose to its climax. In 2001 I was named a minister at the Foreign Office. The Permanent-under-Secretary there, John Kerr, one of the wisest diplomatists in British post-war history, called me up to negotiate my departmental responsibilities. "You've worked in Japan and Korea and Hong Kong, Denis, so you'd better look after that part of the world. There's a bonus. It includes Australia and New Zealand. You speak Spanish so we're going to give you Latin America. But you have to have one tricky region. It's either the Middle East or the Balkans."

In 2001 the Balkans were still considered unfinished business. The Foreign Affairs Select Committee at the House of Commons had produced a highly critical report: it argued that after the initial excitement over the Kosovan conflict the Foreign Office had taken its eye off the ball in the Western Balkans.

Despite the problems and difficulties of today's Europe I remain committed to the politics of the construction of a peaceful, liberal, socially just and open-border Europe. Thus it seemed to me that the political task of trying to engage with the Western Balkans and find ways of helping Croatia and Serbia and Macedonia along the same path to a European Union future that Slovenia had so quietly and effectively began moving along was a worthwhile task for a politician embarking on his first ministerial tour of duty.

As the son of two Catholic parents I have a passionate love affair with the Jewish people just as much as I have given unyielding support to the claims and needs of the many thousands of Kashmiri Muslims who live in my South Yorkshire constituency. In addition I could see myself playing no useful role since the Middle East power players in Jerusalem and the Arab capitals are only interested in the language and policy emanating from the White House. The wishful thinking of European politicians that they could bring much influence to bear on the Middle East was not one I wish to indulge in. So I told Sir John, now Lord Kerr, that I would like to work on the Balkans. It was a decision I never regretted.

I spent the next decade working as a Minister, then as UK delegate to the Council of Europe, and as Prime Minister Blair's personal envoy to Europe working continually in different ways on aspects of Balkan affairs. I hold no particular or personal views on any of the countries or peoples or cultures in the Western Balkans. All the political leaders there have at times inspired me and at times driven me mad with frustration. Some I consider personal friends. Some I admire. Some I think have grown in political leadership and some have become diminished. That is the small change of political life. Sadly, while I speak some Western European languages, I have never found the time to master Albanian, Greek, or the variations of the language that was once known as Serbo-Croat.

Britain is lucky though to have great experts on the contemporary history of all these countries like Noel Malcolm, Misha Glenny, Brendan Simms, James Pettifor, Ian Traynor and Tim Judah and I will make reference later on to other writers whose work is worth examining. Lord Paddy Ashdown, who was named High Representative in Bosnia in 2001, is alongside perhaps Bernard Kouchner, the former French Foreign Minister and before that UN representative in Kosovo, one of the few people who early on recognized the importance of Europe engaging with the Balkans.

Ashdown in particular is the best Foreign Secretary Britain never had. His knowledge and passion for the Western Balkans has made him one of the few British politicians of his generation on whom the term "statesman" might be bestowed. Sadly Ashdown in England and Kouchner in France were not listened to in the wasted years of the early 1990s when European leadership was missing on this issue. But many conversations with them and reading their own exemplary works on the region, and in Kouchner's case his fine account of his period spent in Kosovo, have helped inform my views.

"We must love one another or die," wrote W. H. Auden. Not so. We must live with one another or face misery. I do not want or expect Serbs and Kosovans to love each other. If this short book helps to explain who they are and how they should live with one another it will have served its purpose.

2

Centuries of Kosovo's History

Kosovo has existed for as long as any country in Europe. Like Ireland, Portugal or Latvia it is not one of the half dozen or so big political-geographical European nations and powers that have dominated the continent's history over the last thousand years. As Christopher Hitchens wrote in 1999:

> All through the decades of anti-fascism, anti-Stalinism, anti-colonialism and the battle for "self-determination", in which so many intellectuals either distinguished or disgraced themselves, there was probably no cause with fewer friends than that of Kosovar Albanians.
>
> There was also in all probability, no national minority with a less favourable geopolitical locus. The Basques, the Catholics of Northern Ireland, the Kurds, the minorities at Europe's periphery at least had their partisans and defenders and advocates, and were able to communicate with the outside world. But the Kosovars laboured under a double or triple indemnity. Their past was not understood or examined, their kinship with the strange and inward nation of Albania seemed tribal and bizarre, and they were considered lucky (when they were considered at all) to be enclosed within a state – that of Tito's Yugoslavia – which possessed various "progressive" seals of approval.

Perhaps it is helpful to see Kosovo as the Ireland of the Balkans. Kosovo has always maintained its own identity, its own language, its own sense of its culture and law. Kosovo has all the attributes of a small European nation that has never easily found its way to have its own statehood and identity. This is similar to the case of Ireland, which was invaded and occupied and fought over by England and then invaded and fought over by different religions seeking to exercise supremacy. It was later incorporated into a bigger entity when England and Ireland were merged two hundred years ago and then creating its own sense of national resistance at first peacefully and then after the cruelties of the English oppressor through a short and bloody War of Independence so too. And today there are striking parallels between a Kosovo with complicated, unhappy internal politics, rivalries dating back to the War of Independence, accusations and counter-accusations of killings and politics in which kin and clan play a dominant role just as all these were both accusations and to some extent attributes of Ireland in the first years of its independence.

In the Middle Ages and then under the long era of Ottoman rule the country of Kosovo never had an entirely separate existence. But the same is equally true of Serbia. It is the 19th century that gives birth to the concept of nationhood covering all of Europe not simply the Western European states of France, Britain and Spain. Norway was "part" of Sweden until the early 20th century. The exact and precise frontiers of Poland or Hungary have been as changeable as the wind and currents in the sea. States put together in the rush to draw frontiers after the First World War like Czechoslovakia or Yugoslavia simply crumpled as it was quite clear that that which did not belong together had to come apart. Kosovo itself is a clear geographical entity. It is surrounded by mountains that cut it off from Albania and Macedonia and hills that separate it from the main trade route that runs from Belgrade to Greece and Bulgaria.

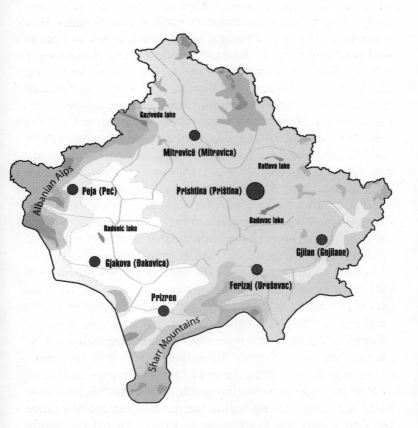

Kosovo has both high rugged mountains and fertile plains producing high quality agricultural products.

It has been continually fought over but remained little known because it had no access to the sea, no major river used for commercial traffic and there was no point in any of the great trade routes of the Balkans having to cross its territory.

The word Kosovo enters European history in the 14th century after the major battle in 1389 at Kosovo Polje just outside today's capital city of Pristina. This was one of a series of battles between the advancing Turks and the retreating Europeans. It was fought on a flat, open field. Unlike the Battle of Poitiers six centuries previously – when Charles Martel stopped the advance of the Moors from Spain, a battle famously described by Gibbon as one that stopped the universities of Europe being converted to Islamic centres of learning – the Battle of Kosovo involved as many Serbs fighting as mercenaries or vassals of the Turkish Sultan with many Albanian Kosovans fighting alongside Prince Lazar. He was the Serb warrior who fell in battle and who in the 19th century was invented as the great Serb hero who had stopped the advance of the Turks further north.

The Sultan Murat also fell in the same battle and it would be more accurate to see it as a 14th-century Battle of the Somme, a bloody encounter with no one clearly winning or losing. But all historians now agree that Kosovans and Serbs were allies against the Ottoman invader. It was only a temporary respite. In 1453, Constantinople fell to the Ottomans who swept on into today's Greece and up the Western Balkans. The conqueror of Constantinople, Sultan Mehmet, moved into the Balkans as he confronted Christian Europe in battle. But this time it was the Serb Prince Djuradj Brankovic who betrayed the armies that had come down from the north to try and staunch the advance of the Turks. The Serb leader accepted bribes from the Ottoman Sultan to allow his forces to move further north in his onslaught on Europe. "The final extinction of the medieval Serbian state" took place in 1459, writes Noel Malcolm. In the 16th and 17th centuries the Turks kept pushing to expand the

Ottoman empire across the Danube and into Alpine Europe. It was not until 1683 that the Turkish advance was finally stopped by the great army led by Poland's King Jan Sobieski outside Vienna.

By then the Ottomans had taken control over much of what today is Serbia, Albania and Macedonia. Whereas the Serbs remained mono-religious, belonging to the Serb Orthodox Church – with its political insistence on identity and honour and rejection of both Catholic and Protestant Christianities – the Kosovans were a mixture of different religions. The Catholic Church remained important. The Albanian Catholic Archbishop Pjeter Bogdani was trained in Rome and wrote the first great literary work in Albanian, *Band of Prophets*, in the late 17th century. He tried to organize a rebellion against Turkish rule in Kosovo in which he lost his life in 1689. The Catholic, Orthodox and small Jewish presence in Kosovo made the nation multi-confessional, which it still is today. Many Albanians, like others living under Ottoman rule, converted to a nominal Islam in order to avoid paying the extra tax that the Ottomans imposed on non-believers. But Ottoman rule was tolerant and providing there was no threat to the Sultan's rule Muslim, Catholic, Unionate, Orthodox and Jewish communities co-existed and were allowed to follow their different faiths until the rise of late 19th and 20th century nationalisms made religious affiliation a matter of national identity and often life or death.

As history unfolded further north and west and as some nations set off on their colonial and imperial adventures the country and people of Kosovo could be said to have slumbered as a backwater both of Europe and the Ottoman Empire. The country was ruled by its own internal law, the legendary *Kanun* (The Code of Lek Dukagjini), which today can be bought in translation anywhere in Albania or Kosovo. It is a strongly worded code of behaviour setting out obligations, duties and punishments. It became the Albanian equivalent of both common and statute law, and a penal code, all written down in one lengthy book. It was written down and made available for translation by a Franciscan friar in the early 20th century. It places immense importance on honour and preserving each family's right to its own status. This justified, and led to, the most terrible blood feuds which continued unchallenged, as the notions of independent law and justice as developed by the political philosophers of England or France or Germany in the 17th and 18th centuries never reached Kosovo or the Western Balkans under Ottoman rule.

Skanderberg (1405–1468) is the national hero for everyone of Albanian origin. His bearded warrior image is found everywhere in Kosovo. He was a hero of Christian Europe as he fought long delaying actions to try and staunch the remorseless Ottoman advance in the Western Balkans. Disraeli wrote a short novel about him and Skanderberg features in Byron's *Childe Harolde*.

Kosovans are steeped in history. They have their heroes like Skanderberg who resisted Ottoman rule in the 15th century. The Kosovan economy ebbed and flowed. Silver mining in Novo Brdo was an important source of wealth in the Middle Ages. This gave way to leather and sheepskin exports and in 1850 an English visitor to the southern Kosovan city of Prizren noted it was well stocked with food shops, a functioning market and some sixty stores selling alcohol. Although nominally Muslim, few Kosovans bother obeying the injunctions against having a glass of wine or something stronger. As Noel Malcolm, the British historian of Kosovo has noted under the Ottoman regime "the Orthodox Churches and the Jews were allowed to maintain their own courts and judges, applying their own laws in their communities in a whole range of civil matters."

The Ottoman rule was based on tolerance of religion provided the areas under their control supplied men in time of war. In fact the transition from Orthodox Serb rule to that of Turks at the end of the Middle Ages almost certainly improved the life of the local population. A peasant, for example, who left his land to become a craftsman in a town could suffer mutilation if his Serb lord objected to losing a rent-producing serf. The Ottoman rulers simply asked for a payment to acknowledge the loss of feudal labour. English folklore as defined by writers of nationalist senti-mentality in the 19th century look back to a sturdy Anglo-Saxon peasantry placed under the cruelties of the Norman Yoke. Robin Hood is the symbol of this mythology. Similarly, the folk memo-ries of Albanians associate Serbs with being cruel masters and the Ottomans as the bearers of a more tempered civilised rule. In truth the Ottomans also helped the Serb Orthodox Church. They restored the Patriarchate to Pec in Kosovo, in 1557.

The question of the religious faith of Kosovans remains a fas-cinating example of European tolerance. When the Jews were expelled by the Catholic monarchs of Spain in 1492 they settled in the Balkans where they survived and flourished under Ottoman rule. While north of the Alps a monumental fight between Cath-olics and Protestants had been dividing Europe for nearly three centuries – and, in the case of Northern Ireland, has yet finally to be settled – the establishment of a cross fertilisation between the two Christian Churches in Kosovo, Islam and Judaism allowed for a great deal of tolerance. What historians of religion called syncretism, a mixing of different faiths and traditions, allowed a great deal of live and let live. The Vatican even created a college in Rome to train priests to go to Kosovo to maintain the Cath-olic faith. The Franciscan friar who travelled to Kosovo in the 17th century complained about "these impious people who said the differences between them and the Christians were small; 'after all,' they said, 'we all have only one God. We venerate your Christ as a prophet and holy man and Mohammed and Christ are brothers.' In the same family one person would be Catholic, one Muslim, and one Orthodox," the friar reported.

3

The Years of Oppression

Kosovo remained an endless source of conflict as it was at the frontier of the permanent struggle for influence in the Western Balkans between the Ottomans and the European powers. In 1822, three thousand Albanian Kosovans tried to walk from Kosovo to Istanbul to present their complaints about the local Ottoman overlord in Pristina. Muslim landowners and Christian notables jointly organized the protest. The Ottoman government refused any self-government to Kosovo but allowed Muslims, Catholics and Orthodox to open schools in the 19th century. As the *Springtime of Nations* took hold in Europe it spread into the Balkans with both Serbs and Albanian Kosovans asserting national identity. The League of Prizren was formed in June 1878. It took control of Kosovo, but as always the fledgling identity of the state found itself crushed between two opposing forces. On one side were the Ottomans under pressure from Russia and Britain, where Gladstone campaigned to throw the Turks 'bag and baggage' out of the Western Balkans. On the other side was Serbia, which was set up as an independent country following the Congress of Berlin in 1878.

The northern European leaders who carved up the failing Ottoman territories in Berlin decided to give Serbia part of Kosovo, which was seen as a minor Albanian-populated Ottoman province. The Serbs immediately set out a policy of ethnic cleansing. According to sources from British National Archives in London, over 150,000 Albanians were forcibly removed from 624 villages during 1878–1879. Muslim Albanian speakers were driven from ancestral lands and villages in southern Serbia just to the east of the current border of Kosovo. Some fifty thousand Albanian-speaking Muslims were resettled in Kosovo. Population surveys of this period give a 70/30% split between Muslim Albanians and

The month long **Congress of Berlin** in the summer of 1878 brought together the then world powers to produce a settlement in Balkans after the conflicts between the Russian and Ottoman empires. Bismarck and Disraeli drew up new frontiers and created new nations but only succeeded in buying a little time before fresh Balkan wars broke out in the early 20th century and the unsolved tensions produced the starting moment for the 1914–1918 War.

Serb Christians, though these numbers would have included some Catholics. Serbia was determined to create an ethnically and religiously pure nation and was happy both to see Albanian speakers displaced towards Kosovo while encouraging the move of Serbs from Kosovo into Serbia proper.

Albanians were inspired by the example set in neighbouring Italy, of a new nation being created. While it was easy to define a geographical Albania based on the Adriatic coastline, the problem of Kosovo remained that it was constantly under pressure from neighbouring countries such as Montenegro, Bulgaria and Serbia looking with greedy eyes at the possibility of incorporating Kosovo into their national territories.

The accelerating disintegration of the Ottoman Empire – reflected in the rise of the so-called Young Turks at the beginning of the 20th century – encouraged Serb ambitions on Kosovo. The Serbs unleashed a propaganda war accusing Kosovans of 'atrocities'. However, the Foreign Office had a Vice Consul W. D. Peckham, who was based in Skopje during 1912–1914. He was the only British diplomat who reported to the Foreign Office about the Serbian manoeuvres. He investigated twelve of these so-called atrocities and noted, "some of the cases reported were untrue and in others the responsibility rests with the Serbs."

Greeks and Bulgarians were also anxious to terminate Ottoman rule in the wider region and joined with Serbia in a war against the crumbling Empire. The Serbs moved swiftly into Kosovo, pushing aside the feeble Ottoman resistance and set about imposing their will on the disarmed Kosovans. The British writer, Edith Durham, who lived in the region during this period, was asked by the British military attaché to visit southern Kosovo to see the aftermath of the 1912 war. The Serbs refused to allow the visit to take place. When she asked why she was banned the conquering soldiers told her, "We have not left a nose on an Albanian there. It's not a pretty sight for a British officer." She later saw soldiers captured by the Serbs whose nose and upper lips had been cut off.

Leon Trotsky was covering the war for a Ukrainian newspaper. As in the 1990s, there was some difference between the regular Serb Army officers and soldiers and the paramilitary units that accompanied them. Trotsky wrote, "Among them were intellectuals, men of ideas, nationalist zealots but … the rest were just thugs, robbers, who had joined the army for the sake of loot." "The Serbs," concluded Trotsky "are engaged quite simply in the systematic extermination of the Muslim population." To its credit, some members of the Serbian Social Democratic Party protested at the mass killing and mutilation of Kosovans. The great pre-1914 Serbian social democrat Dimitrije Tucović had been mobilised as an officer in the 1912 campaign of conquest in Kosovo.

He wrote at the time, "We have carried out the attempted premeditated murder of an entire nation. We were caught in that criminal act and have been obstructed. Now we have to suffer the punishment…. In the Balkan Wars, Serbia not only doubled its territory, but also its external enemies."

Tucović had already crossed swords with the Austrian Marxist social democratic leader, Karl Renner, who supported Vienna's imperial sway over the Western Balkans. Tucovic reminded his Serb readers of Marx's prophetic words, "The nation that oppresses another nation forges its own chains". His appeal had no impact. Nationalist hate whipped up by the Serb Orthodox Church had taken over. In 1913 a Danish journalist reported that five thousand Kosovans had been killed in Pristina after the capture of the city. The Catholic Archbishop of Skopje sent a report to the Vatican about Prizren, although it had peacefully surrendered he noted, "The city seems like the kingdom of death. [The Serbs] knock on the doors of the Albanian houses, take away the men and shoot them immediately... as for plunder, looting and rape, all that goes without saying, henceforth the order of the day is everything is permitted against the Albanians." The Serbs also instigated a programme of forced conversion from Islam to Orthodox Christianity. By this means they hoped to persuade their own public opinion and the outside world that far from being majority Albanian Muslim, Kosovo was full of keen members of the Serb Orthodox Church.

The great powers, including Britain, France, Austria and Hungary, did not want the Serb kingdom to extend to the sea. They recognized and drew up frontiers for a new state of Albania. But Kosovo, lying within its distinct mountain borders, was left at the mercy of Belgrade.

The Treaty of Bucharest, which ended the Second Balkan War of June/July 1913, recognized the annexation by Serbia of Kosovo and Northern Macedonia.

Kosovo was thus incorporated as conquered territory into the Serbian kingdom. The historic home of the Serb Orthodox Church, Pec, was awarded to Montenegro. As Noel Malcolm tartly observes, "There was something paradoxical about this outcome: Serbia had declared to the world that one of its prime reasons for the conquest of Kosovo lay in the historic rights of the Patriarchate of Pec, but it now conceded the seat of the Patriarchate itself to a foreign state." Thus on the eve of the First World War the outlines of today's nation states in the Western Balkans could be seen. While Slovenia, Croatia and Bosnia were still integral parts of the Austrian-Hungarian Empire, Montenegro, Macedonia, Serbia and Greece had all won varying degrees of independence and statehood. Albania also had come into existence, although half of the territory would become parts of Serbia, Montenegro and Greece. The one nation denied its right to exist as an independent entity – Kosovo – lay as a conquered land occupied by Serb invaders.

The cruelty of some Serbs towards the Kosovans continued to worry British officials. The Foreign Secretary, Sir Edward Grey, was sent a note on 6 April 1914 reporting that the Serbians "have resorted to very drastic measures...several villages have been burnt and that in some places wholesale massacres have taken place." Like other reports of Serbian atrocities sent in to Foreign Secretaries in the early 1990s there was no response from London. Serbia and Kosovo were faraway lands. In the spring of 1914 why should a British Foreign Secretary bother himself with quarrels in the Western Balkans?

Kosovo again became a political football between the competing powers in the First World War. The Austro-Hungarian alliance with Bulgaria ensured an easy defeat of the Serbian Army and the occupation of northern Kosovo by Austrian troops and southern Kosovo by Bulgarians. But by 1918 the defeat of these powers was assured. French and Italian soldiers entered Kosovo and handed it back to the Serbs for whose independence and freedom, after all, the First World War had nominally been launched. But no one was available to speak for the independence and freedom of the people of Kosovo.

Although Kosovans tried to get some acknowledgement of their plight at the Paris Peace Conference, the fact that Serbia entered into an agreement with Croatia and Slovenia to form the new Kingdom of Serbs, Croats and Slovenes – later the Kingdom of Yugoslavia – meant no one was interested in the remonstrations of the Kosovans. Albania was not allowed to be present at the Peace Conference. The predominantly Muslim lands in Europe of the former Ottoman Empire were simply disregarded in the carve-up of Europe that took place in Paris between 1918 and 1923. Britain supported irredentist claims by Greece, which came to naught as the new Turkey under Kemal Ataturk came into being.

The Serbs immediately violated the clauses in the newly created League of Nations, which called for the protection of minorities. The Serbs suppressed the Albanian language and tried to impose a Serbian curriculum on Kosovan schoolchildren. Belgrade offered grants of land to Serb colonialist settlers who were prepared to go and live in Kosovo. These crude Serb supremacist policies of colonial settlement were enforced by an occupying Serbian army. The Serb-controlled security apparatus brooked no opposition from Kosovan writers, intellectuals and political activists who sought to keep alive the identity of Kosovo in the aftermath of the First World War.

As the Yugoslav state grew more authoritarian and the anti-Semitic 'Zbor' party grew in strength, Belgrade started to adopt time-honoured ways of holding down the Kosovans. From the mid-1930s, all land was considered the property of the Kingdom of Yugoslavia unless a peasant or local landowner had an official Yugoslav legal document to prove his ownership. Such pieces of paper had never been issued to the Kosovans and dozens of Kosovan villages were handed over to Serb landowners by this trickery. A Serb official noted at the time "Our aim is to make their [the Kosovans'] life impossible and in that way to force them to emigrate." As the Belgrade university historian, Vaso Čubrilović (former member of the Black Hand, the Serbian secret organization responsible for the murder of Austria's

Archduke Franz Ferdinand 28 June 1914 which launched the First World War) argued in 1937: "at a time when Germany can expel tens of thousands of Jews… the shifting of a few hundred thousand Albanian Kosovans will not lead to the outbreak of a world war." He suggested that in Kosovo the Yugoslav state should refuse to recognize old land deeds and dismiss from state and professional service all Kosovans. He also called for "the ill treatment of their clergy, the destruction of their cemeteries and secretly burning down Albanian villages and city quarters."

The Kosovans were also ill-served by the faintly ludicrous Albanian government of King Zog. In order to keep Serb pressure off the country he was turning into a personal fiefdom he refused to allow Kosovans living in Albania to organize openly and had the Kosovan leader Hasan Prishtina assassinated in Greece in 1933. Zog's betrayal of the Kosovans served him ill. Mussolini longed to add new European conquests to the North African territories he had invaded. Mussolini's soldiers attacked Albania in 1939 and Greece in October 1940 and moved into Kosovo after the German Army invaded and conquered Yugoslavia in April 1941. Jews from Serbia fled to Kosovo for protection as Serb anti-Semites collaborated with the German occupiers to send Balkan Jews to the gas-chambers. The American photographer, Norman Gershman, has made a moving documentary evidencing how Kosovan Muslims sheltered the displaced Jews. In the end, though the Jewish communities from Sarajevo to Thessaloniki were destroyed and, in truth, Croats, Serbs, Greeks and Albanians collaborated with the Nazis in the destruction of European Jewry in the region.

4

The Rage of Milošević

After 1945, Kosovo enjoyed a degree of autonomy in Tito's Yugoslavia within the strictly limited freedoms permitted by the regime. Tito's communist ideology understood the difficulty of nationalist sentiment. One of his key political associates, Edvard Kardelj, told the Yugoslav Communist Party Central Committee in the debates in 1945 on the organization of the state that "the best solution would be if Kosovo were to be united with Albania but because neither foreign nor domestic factors favour this, it must remain a compact province within the framework of Serbia."

Kosovo was technically an autonomous province, not a fully-fledged republic, under the Yugoslav Federal Constitution. However, Tito allowed Albanian to be used in Kosovan schools. And he stopped the return of Serb settlers, many of whom had collaborated with the Nazis during Second World War. Nonetheless, the Serb minority remained dominant in Kosovo. Although Serbs amounted to little more than a quarter of the population they used their control of the Communist Party to occupy more than two-thirds of all the administrative positions and in the factories created under Communist plans for industrialisation Serbs made up half of all the employed workers.

As elsewhere in the world the Kosovans had their 1968

movement. In that momentous year demonstrators marched through Pristina calling for Kosovo to be given full status as a republic within the Yugoslav federal system. Other slogans included, "We want a University!" and "Down with colonial policy in Kosovo!" In 1974 a new Yugoslav constitution allowed Kosovo a status equivalent to that of the six national republics within Yugoslavia. Kosovans were allowed to be represented on the collective presidency of Yugoslavia and Kosovans were allowed to draw up their own constitution. The population was growing rapidly. A 1981 census showed that Albanian women in Kosovo gave birth to an average 3.4 children compared to just 1.9 for Serb women in Serbia proper. As Serbs became more and more city and town dwellers in Kosovo their birth rate dropped dramatically and the population imbalance steadily changed in favour of Kosovan Muslim Albanians, many of them peasants as fertile in making children as their soil was fertile in agricultural produce.

In 1980 and 1981 Communist Europe was turned upside down by the creation of Polish Solidarity, a movement of workers, intellectuals, nationalists, religious leaders and students. Yugoslavia after Tito's death was beginning to experience the same movements to end Communist rule that gave rise to Charter 77 in Prague, the Solidarity Movement in Poland and other similar expressions in Hungary and other Communist-controlled regions of Europe. The contagion spread to Kosovo where university students in Pristina in the spring of 1981 protested, demanding freedom. Demonstrations spread all over the country with metal workers joining in – including in the predominantly Serb town of Mitrovica. The name of Adem Demaçi, who like the early Polish founders of Solidarity had called for independence and who had been in prison, was now shouted by Kosovan students. Workers demanded the same freedoms that their comrades in Poland were seeking to achieve. Belgrade crushed the protest, sending in tanks, arresting more than two thousand Kosovans and sentencing them to prison terms of up to fifteen years.

The federal government in Belgrade looked on with dismay at clear indications of the beginning of the end of its rule. The demands of national liberation of the different nations within Yugoslavia from Communist rule grew stronger in the 1980s. What the writer Hariz Halilovic calls "19th century type clero-fascist-nationalism" easily swamped the hopes of a multicultural federation of former Yugoslav nations. As Yugoslav Communist rule evaporated Serb nationalism was matched by its ugly if less murderous equivalent under the Croatian leader Franjo Tudjman. In the 1990s, dressed in his white uniform and reviewing pompous military parades like a latter-day mini-Mussolini, Tudjman also unleashed a wave of vicious ethnic cleansing under war criminals like the former French Foreign Legion soldier, Ante Gotovina. Robin Cook, Britain's former foreign secretary, met Tudjman before the Croat nationalist's death in 1999. "I felt it was the closest I would ever get to talking to a real-life European fascist, full of bombast and national superiority", Cook told me once in the Foreign Office.

Franjo Tudjman (1922–1999) had the good sense to die before he was indicted by the Hague Tribunal. A clerical-nationalist who harked back to the worst episodes of Croatian history, he was the ultra-nationalist President of Croatia after the end of communist Yugoslavia. He cooperated actively with Milošević making a deal with the Serb leader to carve up Bosnia Herzogovina in 1991. Although not on the scale of Serb war crimes, Tudjman's henchmen and paramilitaries shamed European values. The legacy of Tudjman and Milošević continues to deform politics in both Croatia and Serbia.

In 1986 a memorandum was signed by 216 intellectuals, which said the Serbs were suffering 'genocide' in Kosovo. Squabbles and fights between Kosovan Albanians and Serb settlers were seized on by Serb nationalists in Belgrade to present the picture of the Serb nation as suffering under a continual assault from Kosovans. The Serbian Academy of Science presented their Memorandum in 1986 to the Government saying that Belgrade must allow "the return of the exiled people." This extraordinary turning of history on its head, making the Serbs the victims of Kosovan oppression, developed into the "Greater Serbia" nationalism that was finally unleashed at the end of the 1980s.

The Single European Act under the leadership of Jacques Delors, François Mitterrand and Helmut Kohl was heading towards a much greater degree of integration following the transformation of a limited free trade area into what became, after the 1992 Maastricht Treaty, the European Union. As the disintegration of Communist Europe accelerated in the mid-1980s, leaders – whether currently in government or in opposition – of countries trying to work out their future had a choice. They could aim for closer alignment with the European Community. Or they could move from Communist authoritarianism to nationalist authoritarianism and stake a claim to national leadership based not on European values but rather a reversion to the ancient nationalist spirits of their people.

In different forms, that contest between a European and a nationalist future dominated the politics of post-Communist Europe in the period after the end of Communism. It still reverberates today as some of the political debates in Hungary, the Baltic States and in Poland, under the Kaczyński twins, have demonstrated. (The rise of ugly xenophobic nationalism is also evident in Western Europe as the rise of populist identity nationalist politics indicates.) Christopher Hitchens wrote of the 'national socialist' project that began to consume Serbia in particular and found its embodiment in Slobodan Milošević. He was a junior energetic member of the Central Committee of the Serbian Communist Party. He had never shown any interest in Kosovan affairs in his climb up the political ladder of the Serb Communist apparatus. But history finds people, both good and bad, to drive the historical process forward. In Milošević, the Kosovans found a Serb politician not seeking to exercise a loose tolerant sovereignty over the people of Kosovo but someone who decided to make it his life's work to crush the very spirit of the Kosovan people.

On 24 April 1987, Milošević went to speak to Serbs in Kosovo Polje – the scene of the famous battle of 1389. Local Serb trouble-makers brought up trucks filled with stones. Angry Serbs demanded tougher action against the Albanian majority in Kosovo. Milošević came out from the meeting he was holding to talk to the crowd who had been pushed and shoved by the local police. Serb television news cameras were there to capture Milošević shouting at the crowd, "No one should dare to beat you!" He made a rabble-rousing speech talking of the sacred rights of the Serb people. It was not in the Communist tradition of pedantic bureaucratic text read out word for word from a written typescript. The crowd started chanting his name – "Slobo, Slobo!" The speech extolling Serb nationalism and the promise that the Serbs would never give an inch to the majority population of Kosovo was played again and again on Serb television.

Overnight Milošević became a national hero for the Serbs. He continued to whip up nationalist feeling against Kosovans. Milošević organized a rally in Belgrade attended by 350,000 people at which he explained his creed. "Every nation has a love which eternally warms its heart. For Serbia it is Kosovo." He went on to propose changes to the constitution which would remove from the autonomous Kosovo Assembly rights over police, courts, and even the choice of language to be used for state documents and teaching in schools. It was clear to the people of Kosovo that Milošević's Yugoslav Communism was morphing into an ugly Serb nationalism.

Further north in Poland in 1988 a wave of strikes and

occupations of mines were putting pressure on the Communist rulers there. In Kosovo it was workers and students who took the lead as the miners at Trepca went on hunger strike and barricaded themselves in the mines in protest at the Serb efforts to crush their identity. The Serb response was more repression with armoured cars sent to surround the Kosovan Assembly and Milošević organising a huge celebration for the 600th anniversary of the Battle of Kosovo Polje. Twenty-five thousand policemen from Serbia were sent into Kosovo. In 1990 Milošević closed the Kosovo Academy of Arts and Sciences and the main Albanian language newspaper. Thousands of Kosovans who worked for the civil service and in other state jobs were fired.

The invasion of Kuwait by Saddam Hussein was absorbing the majority of the international community's attention at this time. The main preoccupation of European and international policy makers in the Balkan region was focused on developments further north in the rapidly disintegrating Yugoslavia: the decision of Slovenia and then Croatia to leave the Yugoslav Federation. No one much noticed what was happening in Kosovo.

As with Václav Havel in Prague or Bronislaw Geremek and Tadeusz Mazowiecki in Poland the resistance to Serb nationalist oppression was organized by intellectuals and writers, namely the Association of Philosophers and Sociologists of Kosovo and the Association of Writers of Kosovo. Four hundred thousand people signed a petition "For Democracy, Against Violence." A literary critic, Dr Ibrahim Rugova, who had written on the 17th-century Kosovan Catholic Archbishop Pjeter Bogdani, emerged as the leader of this peaceful protest movement. I met Rugova many times before his death. He was gentle, unaggressive, courteous and as apolitical a politician as I have ever met before or since in Europe. We always spoke in French as for many of the Albanian intelligentsia of his generation it was to France and French that they looked for inspiration more than English. He was a slight man who never raised his voice. In a curious public relations move he gave a piece of rock from the ground of Kosovo to every visitor who came to see him in Pristina. For Rugova it was a physical symbol of his attachment to his nation. In December 1989 he helped found the Democratic League of Kosovo which as Noel Malcolm writes "came to function, rather like Solidarity in Poland, as a cross between a party and a mass movement". It had a claimed membership of 700,000 in the 1990s.

Serb discrimination and oppression of the Kosovan Albanians continued aggressively throughout the 1990s. Most Kosovan doctors were dismissed from hospitals. Six thousand schoolteachers were fired in 1990. A new Serb curriculum, which excluded Albanian literature and history was imposed on schools. People were arrested and imprisoned on the accusation that they had insulted "the patriotic feelings of Serbs."

Rugova created a parallel society in which Kosovan school children were taught in their own language and health clinics were opened to treat Kosovans denied health care by the Serbs. As Milošević declared war to protect Serb interests in Croatia and Bosnia the international communities' economic sanctions against Belgrade hit Kosovo hard. Two hundred and fifty thousand Kosovans had to depend on food parcels distributed by charities and as access to medical care was restricted death from measles and polio amongst Kosovan children rose. Serb warlords like Arkan were elected to the Serb National Assembly to represent a Kosovo

Željko Ražnatovió, commonly know as '**Arkan**', was assasinated in 2000 before he could be brought to justice; he was wanted for crimes against humanity. His paramilitary force, 'The Tigers', was responsible for some of the most brutal aspects of ethnic cleansing during the Balkan Wars and he achieved iconic status among both Serbians and their enemies.

constituency, so cynical had the political elites in Belgrade become. Arkan said that the Kosovans were simply temporary incomers and the nation really was Serb at heart. Street names in Kosovan towns were changed to commemorate Serbian historic figures and saints. And in the manner of earlier colonial attempts Serbs were offered five hectares of Kosovan land if they agreed to move into Kosovo and settle there.

5

Europe Wakes Up, Slowly

Kosovans voted with their feet. More than 500,000 had fled as refugees to northern Europe by 1993. In my own constituency of Rotherham in South Yorkshire there are still a number of Kosovan asylum seekers. Switzerland faced the biggest ever migration of asylum seekers in its history – far bigger than the flow of Jews from Nazi Germany in the 1930s.

The rise of Serb nationalism coupled with UN economic sanctions against Belgrade with the unsuccessful objective of discouraging the Serb war machine in Croatia and Bosnia opened the way to the criminalisation of the Western Balkan economy and Kosovo was no exception.

Some of it was openly encouraged by Serb authorities using warlords like Arkan. Kosovan and Albanian gangs also got in on the act. Montenegro, as Misha Glenny has written in his book *McMafia*, depended almost entirely for its revenue on the smuggling of cigarettes, which were sent by fast motorboats across to Italy to be sold as contraband. This illegal trade, however, went much further than cigarettes. The criminal world's supply of drugs, trafficked sex slaves and cigarettes was in response to ever-increasing demand from the rest of Europe. As Glenny writes: "Nor did the Serbs and Montenegrins have a monopoly on all these activities…Organized crime is such a rewarding industry in the Balkans because ordinary Western

Europeans spend an ever burgeoning amount of their spare time and money sleeping with prostitutes; smoking untaxed cigarettes; sticking €50 notes up their noses; employing illegal untaxed immigrant labour on subsistence wages; or purchasing the livers and kidneys of the desperately poor in the developing world."

One of the most troubling aspects of the Milošević era's induced criminalisation was the rise in people-trafficking. As John Davies of the Sussex University Centre for Migration Research showed in his study of prostituted Albanian women trafficked into France, the women presented themselves as Kosovans. The reason for this identity switch was that the case for granting Kosovans asylum in the face of Serb oppression was widely accepted by the end of the 1990s. This trafficking extended also to the sale of human organs. This disgusting practice fuelled by the demand of elderly rich people for a fresh kidney to try and ward off the pain of kidney disease sunk roots in the region.

The Western powers could only deal with one crisis at a time. The Serb brutalities in Bosnia including the siege of Sarajevo and then the cold-blooded murder of over 8,000 European Muslims at Srebrenica in 1995 gripped all the Western policy makers' imaginations. In this massacre the resources of the Serb state were placed at the disposal of the murderers. 8,000 blindfolds were prepared as were 8,000 lengths of wire to tie the victims' hands. Hundreds of buses were commandeered to take the victims to stadiums. Two thousand willing Serb executioners took five days, working overtime to complete the mass murder in July 1995. One participant, Drazen Erdemovic, told The Hague tribunal "I couldn't shoot anymore, my index finger started to go numb from so much killing, I was killing them for hours."

In the House of Commons the Conservative Government Ministers found endless excuses not to intervene in the Western

Balkans. I sat as a newly elected MP listening to the then Conservative Foreign Secretary, Sir Malcolm Rifkind, making a statement on Srebrenica and refusing to lift a finger to intervene. Other MPs, including to their shame some Labour MPs, told him to ignore the "something must be done brigade." I felt as if I had been transported back to the House of Commons of the 1930s as the Apostles of Appeasement of Hitler explained why Britain should not intervene to stop the march of fascism in Europe or Spain culminating in the shame of the Munich Agreement. British Conservatives were continually on the wrong side of history in this period. As the new post-Communist European states looked to join both the European Union and NATO the Defence Secretary, Sir Malcolm Rifkind, explained in 1993 to a Russian audience that Britain would resist German plans for NATO expansion.

A year later, the Foreign Secretary, Douglas Hurd, said that "what NATO has been doing for the United Nations in Bosnia is not part of its basic task and is not a test of its worth." To be fair to the British Conservatives they were not alone. In all Western capitals there was a lack of any imaginative policy about what was at stake as the Serb murder machine rolled all over the former Yugoslavia. I had been close to many of those who secured Bill Clinton's victory in 1992 and in March 1993 was having lunch in the White House mess with one of Clinton's closest advisers. I said that European feebleness on the Balkans would inevitably require the commitment of the United States. "Let me tell you one thing, Denis," the White House policy maker firmly told me: "This democratic president will never send a single US soldier to the Balkans. That is the Europeans' back yard and Europe will have to clear up the mess."

European hubris was on display in 1992 when the Luxembourg Foreign Minister, Jacques Poos, speaking on behalf of EU member states said that "the hour of Europe has sounded" as he pledged action to stop the Serb nationalist onslaught on innocent civilians in Sarajevo. Luxembourg, which is best known as the European Union's onshore tax haven with its banking secrecy protecting the wealth of its clients, was not exactly a military or foreign policy mover and shaker. In fact it required a turnaround of public opinion and leadership in the United States and the growing acceptance of what the French socialist, Bernard Kouchner called "*le droit d'ingérence*" – the right to intervene – as a new philosophy guiding international action to grow in strength before effective action was taken to stop the murderous tactics of Milošević in Bosnia.

The view that military intervention to stop Milošević was wrong was widespread. In the House of Commons in May 1995, Sir Peter Tapsell, the veteran Conservative MP who had served as a political aide to Anthony Eden at the time of the Suez crisis, asked: "Why are we not sending troops to Angola, Rwanda, Cambodia, Kurdistan, Tibet and Chechnya, to mention just a few. What is so very different about Bosnia?" There were Labour MPs like Robert Wareing, known in the Commons as the Honourable Member for Belgrade, who took a similar line. Other Labour MPs who rose to high office under Tony Blair were also Serb apologists.

Paddy Ashdown, leader of the Liberal Democrats, as well as mainstream Labour leaders, tried to put the appeasement policy of the Conservatives under pressure. The Labour leader, John Smith, insisted in May 1993 that "if the Serbs are to be stopped, they must be given an ultimatum that is backed by a credible threat to their lines of communication and supply in Bosnia." These lessons were to be absorbed by Tony Blair when he succeeded John Smith as Labour leader and Robin Cook when he became Foreign Secretary. In the earlier 1990s, however, there was a reluctance of the main opposition party to break ranks with the Conservative Government on a major international policy issue. Shadow Labour Foreign Secretaries think they sound like statesmen if they echo the Government line. But the job of an opposition is to oppose. The failure of Labour to think clearly about the failures of John Major's policy in the Balkans left Britain always one step behind, rather than shaping events.

Public opinion was confused. Many commentators were still living under previous codes, which saw the conflict in the Western Balkans not as a war of nationalist aggression but as an unpleasant internal conflict, which would be solved locally without any great need for the democratic world to intervene. No one seemed to notice that Britain's domestic politics and sense of balance and equilibrium were now coming under massive pressure from the waves not just of Kosovan asylum seekers but from other economic migrants. These, in addition to trafficked or smuggled people from many different parts of the world, were able to use the chaos and confusion in the Western Balkans to join the great organized routes of trafficking and people smuggling that brought hundreds of thousands of incomers to Britain with consequences that the nation is still living with. So at a crude domestic policy-making level it would have made sense to step in and try and restore order in the Western Balkans at a much earlier stage.

Kosovo simply lay unnoticed. In one of his last acts as US President before handing over to Bill Clinton after the latter's election victory in November 1992, President George Bush issued a Christmas warning saying that Milošević should not start a war in Kosovo and assume that America would not react. President Bush had sent a thousand US troops to Macedonia the year before where they acted as a kind of trip-wire to prevent Milošević extending Serb nationalist aggression south into Macedonia. Their presence did not in itself bring peace and harmony between the Albanian and Macedonian-speaking inhabitants of the country but they at least prevented open war breaking out. Bush tried to make the same point about Kosovo but a British official representing the Conservative-controlled

Foreign Office denounced Bush's statement as "a unilateral warning given by the US administration without consultation as far as I know and certainly without seeking to get our support." Moreover, added the British diplomat as he sneered at the foresight of the US president, the US warning: "had no UN validation." How right Bush was and how sad that no British or European official had such clarity of vision.

Despite their indictment, Karadžić and Mladić eluded arrest and transfer to the Hague for years after Dayton. It was an open secret in Belgrade that Mladić was protected by former army comrades. He and his family received a pension even though he was wanted as a war criminal. **Karadžić** was arrested in 2008 and his trial on accusations of genocide was still under way at time of writing. **Mladić** was detained in 2011, 16 years after his indictment. Despite protestations by Serb politicians that they sincerely wanted to send Karadžić and Mladić to the Hague, many questioned how diligent the manhunt was and how the detentions happened at a time convenient to ruling politicians in Belgrade.

In his masterly philippic about British appeasement of Milošević, *Unfinest Hour. Britain and the destruction of Bosnia*, Professor Brendan Sims of Cambridge University details the failure of John Major's enfeebled administration to offer any leadership, take decisions, forge a coalition, apply effective military force, or even have the basic policy understanding to realize what was at stake in the Western Balkans both in terms of international policy and in the encouragement of mass migration and asylum seeker flows. The former US Ambassador to NATO, Robert Hunter, has gone further and accused British ministers of actively blocking all UN and NATO efforts to stop the Serb war in Bosnia between 1993 and 1995.

Some Conservative MPs like Sir Patrick Cormack, now Lord Cormack, did speak out. So did the leading Conservative backbencher William Cash, who criticized his own government's policy. But Cash was so obsessed with promoting his campaign against Britain being in the European Union that he failed to realize his support for a nation-first politics in Britain meant if literally applied that Europe would not be able to intervene in Bosnia. Sims' fine book, which should be read by all foreign policy makers, has only two passing references to Kosovo. The war in Bosnia finished with the Dayton accords followed by the indictment of Radovan Karadžić and Ratko Mladić by the war crimes tribunal set up in The Hague. Richard Holbrooke, the American diplomatist who negotiated the Dayton agreement, agreed to Radovan Karadžić's demand that the settlement should not cover Kosovo. This failure of diplomacy left for another day, and another war, the question of Kosovo.

6

A War of Liberation

After the Dayton settlement the world hoped the Balkans would return to peace. British diplomats in charge of the failed Balkan policy of the Conservative government under the weak John Major went off into the City to work as financial brokers for Milošević.

The democratic world hoped that Serb nationalism had been finally stopped. It misunderstood the true nature of the fusion of nationalist and Communist authoritarianism that Slobodan Milošević embodied. Having been thwarted in Bosnia he now turned his attention to Kosovo. He wanted a final solution there that would satisfy Serb nationalist feeling.

In 1996, the Kosovan leader, Ibrahim Rugova, mistakenly sensing that Kosovo's moment was approaching and still hoping for a peaceful way to national self-determination, offered to negotiate face-to-face with Milošević. Bravely – if to the dismay of many Kosovans – he shelved his pre-condition of recognition for Kosovo and agreed a deal with Milošević so that school and higher-education property would be made available for teaching students in Albanian. But Milošević refused to implement the agreement. Instead, in 1997 the Serb police beat up Kosovan students who organized a march in Pristina demanding the right to attend their own university.

The British Defence Secretary, George Robertson, told the

House of Commons that both Ratko Mladić and the paramilitary leader 'Arkan' Željko Ražnatović, had been recruited by the Belgrade leadership to command and supply units responsible for massacring and raping thousands of ethnic Albanians in Kosovo. 'Arkan' who nominally represented a Kosovan constituency, publicly mobilised his private army – the 'Tigers' – to fight in Kosovo.

Milošević banned outside reporters from visiting Kosovo in the hope that such censorship would remove Kosovo as an international issue. Serb forces were now running amok as Milošević increased the tempo of terror to break the will of the Kosovan people. Dozens of people were killed in different attacks in 1998.

Rugova, meanwhile, had presided over the creation of a parallel organization of political parties, businesses, schools, universities, publishing and healthcare in the 1990s. It was Kosovo's authentic civil society within the formal shell of a Serb-administered state. Economists have argued that the creation of a more free-market enterprise outlook as part of a parallel economy (helped by links to the growing Kosovan diasporas in Switzerland, Germany, Italy, France and Britain) helped wean Kosovans away from a statist, government-controlled outlook on business. Certainly, the Kosovo of 2011 has the look and feel of a raw, upstart, anything-goes kind of economy. But in the period after Dayton, Rugova

The paradox of the former Yugoslavia and the tragedy of Kosovo lay in the wide range of governance that might have been offered to Kosovo before the final conflict in 1999. There is a rich menu of entities with a clear national status like Catalonia, Quebec, Scotland or South Tyrol which live within a broader sovereign framework of Spain, Canada, Britain and Italy respectively. Had Kosovo been granted such status in the 1980s or 1990s, as Rugova sought a peaceful compromise for the war of 1999, the mass expulsions and refugee flows, and the current stale-mate might well have been avoided.

was unable to persuade his Serb overlords to allow Kosovo even that amount of freedom, autonomy, or a status similar to that of Catalonia in Spain or Quebec in Canada.

In the 1990s the writer and activist Christopher Hitchens met Rugova at the Carnegie Endowment in Washington. Hitchens noted that the Kosovan leader's seminar "did not magnetise the sort of attention that is created by the visit of a 'freedom fighter' or *guerrillero*. The very meekness of the Kosovans seemed to condemn them to obscurity, whereas any show of obduracy on their part would revive the classical stereotypes that were used to defame them." By the end of the 1990s that meekness had come to the end of the road, when the Kosovan people decided enough was enough, and the days of oppression by Serbia could not continue.

As Misha Glenny wrote in his masterly *The Balkans 1804–1999* (in 1998, before the international community's intervention),

> The Kosovo Albanians looked northwards to Croatia and Bosnia with envy. They observed that with the help of the international community, the Serbs had been defeated completely in the former and partially in the latter. In Bosnia-Hercegovina, the international community had pledged $5 billion to aid reconstruction. Despite being Milošević's first victim, the (Kosovan) Albanians had received nothing. As long as they remained passive, the more radical Albanians reasoned, the outside world would ignore them, the Milošević regime could continue to deny Albanian rights and his shabby regime of repression would continue.

Glenny had an acute political feel for what was about to happen.

Tim Judah is another of the fine writers in English on Kosovo. As a correspondent he saw how Rugova's pacifism morphed into a more muscular search for national liberation. Rugova's peaceful approaches were unrewarded by Milošević or the West. In 2001 Tudah described the appearance of the Kosovan Liberation Army (KLA) thus: "It is hardly an exaggeration to say that the Kosovan Liberation Army must rank as one of the most successful guerrilla organizations of modern times – especially since it has never won a battle." Judah describes how a group of young men, some of them with a primitive left-over Marxist-Leninism from university days, some like Hashim Thaçi, a student in Zurich, others like Ramush Haradinaj, based in Kosovo, decided that the time had come to move from Rugova's passive resistance to armed resistance. As in Ireland in 1916, the decision to use weapons and strike at what was seen as an occupying state had terrible consequences.

In 1997, Albania had been rocked by an economic-financial crisis as a pyramid selling scheme in which hundreds of thousands of Albanians had placed their savings collapsed. There was chaos in the country and a political crisis took hold as the state lost all authority. One consequence was that the Kosovo-Albanian border opened and it was possible to obtain weapons, ammunition and create arms caches for the fledging KLA, in the manner of the IRA using Ireland to hide its guns and gunmen in the war with Britain in the 1970s and 1980s. Unlike Ireland, the war in Kosovo was over almost as soon as it begun.

In 1998 an attack by young KLA militants drove Serb army units out of western Kosovo, close to the Albanian border. Milošević ordered a savage riposte and in the summer and autumn of 1998 Serb tanks, artillery and soldiers reduced Kosovan towns and villages to rubble with 250,000 homeless people living rough in the hills, all looking to flee Serb brutality as asylum seekers. Tony Judt, in his magisterial *Postwar: A History of Europe Since 1945*, has no hesitation in writing of "Milošević's continued mistreatment – massacres – of the Albanians in Kosovo." The TV images forced foreign ministries to react and the US threatened Belgrade with air strikes. As Serb troops withdrew under this pressure, the KLA reappeared, rather like French *résistants* emerging from the maquis in the second half of 1944 to take over the towns evacuated by the retreating Germans.

But the Serbs did not see themselves as Germans, and still saw Kosovo as part of their heritage. Sporadic fighting broke out. The KLA sought to group themselves into a more coherent force. Natural military leaders like 31-year-old Ramush Haradinaj emerged. His book, *A Narrative of War and Freedom*, is a classic in the genre of underground resistance-cum-liberation literature. Its cover has Haradinaj posing in camouflage uniform like an army leader. For the outside world, the story was just another tsunami of asylum seekers being forced to leave Kosovo.

Rugova, the pacifist critic of literature who had become Kosovo's symbolic leader, was sidelined by young men like Haradinaj and Hashim Thaçi, a political science student in exile at Zurich University. James Pettifer who has travelled in and written widely on Kosovo, noted that Thaçi's 30th birthday fell in April 1999. The KLA leader was slim, good-looking, well-dressed in a blue suit and with a mobile phone to hand as he met Western diplomats. Pettifer described how Thaçi could "discuss Mill or Thomas Hobbes with the fluency of an Oxford PPE graduate. But his other name is 'Snake', and he is a natural, elemental force from the Kosovo countryside, a rural revolutionary who seeks to destroy Serbian rule."

As Charles Crawford, the able former ambassador to Belgrade likes to say, "You can lead the Serbs to water but you cannot make them think." Milošević had a partner for peace in Ibrahim Rugova. But to paraphrase another witticism from corridors of geo-political negotiations: the Balkan conflicts (then and today) have been dominated by political leaders in Belgrade who never miss an opportunity to miss an opportunity.

Milošević wasted a decade when he might have come to a deal with Rugova.

In Thaçi, who had been declared Kosovan Prime Minister-in-exile by a provisional committee based in Tirana, he faced a younger, more energetic leader. But the real threat Milošević faced was that the democratic world would no longer tolerate his oppression and wanted an end once and for all to his murder machine. After a decade of mainly Serb-initiated killings and war in the Western Balkans someone, somewhere had to say enough was enough. A new generation of social democratic leaders – Tony Blair in Britain, Lionel Jospin in France, Gerhard Schröder in Germany, Massimo d'Alema in Italy – had taken over from the tired conservatives like Helmut Kohl and John Major.

Milošević was given the last chance at the Rambouillet conference, when the democratic world tried for the last time to persuade the Serb leader to change policy in the Balkans. It was in vain. Where he had failed to break the will of the people of Bosnia, Milošević felt he could still dominate Kosovo and intimidate its people. In January 1999 Serb paramilitaries went on the rampage in Racak killing 45 and wounding many more. Television showed rows of mutilated Kosovan bodies. William Walker was the US ambassador who headed the peace-keeping mission sent in by the OSCE (Organisation for Security and Cooperation in Europe) to try and stop the fighting. He described the Racak incident as a war crime, with the clear implication that the Serb leaders were now being seen no longer as state leaders willing to negotiate a settlement but as brutes that were moving themselves beyond the limits of acceptable political behaviour in Europe.

As the world looked on with horror at the Serb massacres, 'Arkan', flanked by his Tiger bodyguards, swaggered through the Belgrade hotels where the international journalists were based, insisting the entire fault lay with the Kosovans and that the Serbs had nothing to apologise for. His bombast counted for little as the world watched the columns of refugees leaving Kosovo in an exodus without parallel in Europe for generations. Finally, the patience of the democracies ran out.

The elaboration of new doctrines about the international community's responsibility to protect and its right to intervene provided the philosophical basis for the military intervention, even without a UN resolution. UN law is defined by the political priorities of the Permanent Members of the UN Security Council. They are not a supreme court of disinterested judges applying commonly accepted law.

For the Communist dictatorship of China, or the increasingly authoritarian, anti-American and anti-EU Russia, there were no circumstances in which their internal ideological outlook would permit a UN resolution to tackle Milošević. The Russian Orthodox Church had resumed its clerical-political role. Russia had always regarded the Balkans as its backyard, following the great Russian campaigns against Ottoman rule in the 19th century.

The talks at Rambouillet would only have succeeded if Milošević had been ready to cut a deal. But buoyed by Russian backing to stop any UN resolution that permitted UN troops to take over military and security control in Kosovo, the Serb leader decided he could face down the democratic world. He was wrong.

Tony Blair elevated himself to the rank of world leader as he put together a coalition to stop Milošević and coaxed a reluctant President Clinton to use the full panoply of US military might. The NATO air strikes began in March 1999 and the following month Blair made a speech in Chicago which set out his doctrine on the existence of an 'international community' and its right and duty to intervene to stop the relentless abuse of human rights by leaders like Milošević and his henchmen.

Under Blair's energetic leadership the West was not going

to make the same mistake as the Euro Atlantic leadership in the early 1990s when British ministers actively blocked the use of international force to stop Milošević. By 1999, NATO was involved in the first bombardment of a European capital city since 1945. An invading army was put together. World affairs became dominated by a faraway land most had never heard of.

In the House of Commons I worked as a political aide in the Foreign Office. My diary notes from this period show how the Kosovo crisis was mounting. It begins with an emergency debate after NATO began its air campaign on 24 March 1999.

The talks at **Rambouillet** in February and March 1999 were intended to persuade Serbia to turn away from its repression and killings in Kosovo. The US, France, Britain, Serbia and Kosovo met to try and reach an agreement to avoid full-scale military intervention. Serbia refused to accept that international peacekeepers would have to enter Kosovo to protect civilians. Paradoxically, under the terms of the proposed Rambouillet agreement Kosovo would have remained linked to Serbia but with considerable autonomy. Belgrade rejected this compromise. Unless it was prepared to capitulate to Milošević the West had no choice but to resort to force to make Serbia let the Kosovans be free.

Thursday, 25 March 1999

All afternoon there had been a debate on Kosovo, which was opened by Robin Cook and closed by George Roberson so I didn't have to stay there the whole time. Tony Benn made an absolutely ludicrous speech but he was countered by Ken Livingstone and so far, the clear majority is in favour of what we are doing. There is almost a generational divide between younger Labour MPs who are ready to see action taken and the older gang who have not got any bearings since the end of the Cold War and for whom anything that involves the United States is completely intolerable and must be opposed.

As George Robertson came to the end of his wind up speech, Tony Benn rose just after six and sought to move to a vote. But again this was a fake move. Although one or two people shouted "No" with him, no one was willing to force a division and see how many people would actually go through the lobby against intervention. It was shabby, cheap parliamentary procedure in which the impression is given that the government is preventing a vote taking place, when in fact the vote can take place quite easily, provided four of those opposed are willing to act as tellers. I doubt if Benn had four people who really believe in anything he says any more.

Wednesday, 31 March 1999

Robin is to speak at the Parliamentary Labour Party on Kosovo, where he denounces "genocide and ethnic cleansing". I wish he wouldn't use the word genocide. It trips too easily off the lips but the one thing Milošević is not doing is going in for mass extermination, despite the evil brutality of his troops on the ground.

"I was reluctant to get into this military action," said Cook. "For over seven weeks we worked hard to a peace plan. It would have provided integrity for Serbia. Russian negotiators were blunt in blaming the Serbian side. Milošević believes his own lies. When he saw Richard Holbrook he told him that there was no fighting going on in Kosovo, it had all been invented by the media."

Robin keeps insisting that no ground troops will be sent. David Winnick, ever the anti-fascist, asks about bringing Milošević to justice, but how on earth is this going to happen if there is to be no proper invasion of Serbia and conquest of its dictator?

The Committee Room is fairly empty to begin with; it fills up a bit as Robin is speaking but there is no sense of urgency, anger, or anything much but a sense of some puzzlement and worry that everything is so unclear on the ground. As always, it will be the facts established from the bellies of aeroplanes, or the movements of public opinion around the world, or the fighting cruelties of different troops that decide things, not really what is said here today.

Monday, 5 April 1999
Easter Monday and the story is of thousands and thousands and thousands of refugees being driven from Kosovo. Is this what Milošević wants – a partition of Kosovo with the mines and the monasteries being attached to Serbia? The reports of human tragedy not seen in Europe since the great deportations of Germans from Silesia and the other movements after the war are just too awesome. Politics have somehow become more important than economics. I hope this gives the political class in the democracies the confidence to take stronger decisions to ensure that the economic forces which have been extremely unfavourable to Serbia are now brought more properly under control.

Thursday, 8 April 1999
I talked to Nick Cohen who phoned me from The Observer *wanting to know my views on the sending of ground troops. I told him that I thought there would be no difficulty from the Labour Party or public opinion which, if anything, has hardened in favour of what NATO and the Governments are doing. Milošević may have thought he would divide Western public opinion but instead his own stupidity has hardened it to the point where it is almost difficult to imagine negotiating with him were he to offer to meet allied terms tomorrow. I have now been reading* Le Monde *for a week and it is like seeing in one week a century's worth of French debates about foreign policy.*

Tuesday, 13 April 1999
Back to the Commons for Blair's statement on Kosovo. It was restrained and professional. William Hague gave a dutiful measure of support but on the front bench to his left and right, and on the back benches behind one could sense the discomfort and unhappiness at the fact that it was a Labour Government running a high profile war. Only mavericks like Alan Clark came out formally to criticize the bombing of 'Christian' people. From

*our side Tam Daylell made a rather good point about the crimi-
nal and mafia style of much the Albanian Diaspora and the KLA.
We are supporting some very unsavoury people. But that's war. It
recasts relations continuously.*

*I went with Joyce Quin (the Europe Minister) in the car back
to the Commons for a PLP Foreign Affairs Committee meeting
on Kosovo, which Robin addressed. The Committee Room was
jammed but he gave a good performance and I thought looked
fresher and less tired than I would have expected given the pressure he must be under. He thrives on this kind of crisis – it is an
absolute drug for him. The questioning wasn't very purposeful and
the support was fairly clear, but very conditional and unhappy. I
cannot think of a war where there has been so little enthusiasm,
jingoism or sense of achievement. It is a funny war in which a
Christian coalition bombs other Christians to protect Muslims.
Or perhaps it is the first socialist war in which the means of production are destroyed but the working class, as far as possible, is
left intact.*

Monday, 19 April 1999

*In the Commons, the debate on Kosovo starts pronto at 3.30. Cook
opens in his usual competent style but one or two of his jibes,
which normally would get under the skin of the Tories and raise
cheers on our side, don't work. Kosovo has completely divided the
political class. It is obvious that the Tories want Blair to fall flat on
his face, just as the right in America wants to see Clinton make a
fool of himself. It will be the complete vindication of the view that
the 1968 generation of leaders are simply airheads, flaky spin-
doctors unable to grapple with the big decisions of high politics.*

Thursday, 22 April 1999

*I go on to the Channel 4 mid-morning TV programme about
Kosovo and waffle away echoing the government's position. Why
are our military so incompetent? We now have the NATO fiftieth*

anniversary celebrations in Washington, but there is nothing to toast at all. I fear this war will do no good at all, even if we can spin a victory out of it. God knows what it is costing.

Thursday, 29 April 1999

I drove up to Coventry for an evening meeting at Coventry Trades Council on the war.

It was ghastly. I had forgotten how many manic Trot and Maoist groups still existed. Tariq Ali and an SWP woman were against the war and Anthony Arblaster and I argued the intervention case. The arguments are not new, but the atmosphere is turning sour. There are too many attacks on civilian targets. As I parked the car near the Methodist Cathedral Hall in the middle of Coventry I noticed some big burly middle-aged men with shoulders and necks of about equal size. There were all wearing "Stop the War" t-shirts. In the Hall they sat in the front and my worst fears were realized when I worked out I had an audience that in addition to aggressive Blair-hating Trots consisted of immigrant Serb workers who had arrived in Coventry over the years as economic refugees.

They heard out my speech in silence until I got to the bit about rape when they exploded with shouts of "Dirty lies... CIA propaganda...! Why you no tell the truth...?"

The chairman, a nice academic who heads the local trades council, jumped up to try and restore calm, but it was useless. I stood my ground and finished my speech but one could see the raw, naked, nationalist hate and passion. If it was like this here, with a dozen of them in Coventry, God knows what it must be like in Serbia. A young man at the back stood up and announced that he was Albanian and talked about self-determination, independence for the Kosovar people and the need to arm the KLA. The Serb workers at the front started to explode and one took off his jacket as if he wanted to go back and kill the Albanian with his bare hands. I suppose it would be like putting ultra-Orange Unionist working class sectarians with their opposites from the

Nationalist Sinn Fein community and expecting them to get on. What a dreadful business!

Arblaster, who is a traditional lefty and teaches politics at Sheffield University, said that he had opposed the Falklands War, and the Iraq War, but this one was a just war. This showed the extent to which the left is split on this. I was glad when it was over and I could leave these horrible Serbian gastarbeiters behind. I gave Arblaster a ride back to Sheffield and collapsed tired over some fish and chips at home at about 11.30.

Monday, 10 May 1999

I go back to the House to try and whip up interest for Robin's statement.

Robin plunges into a statement about war atrocities and how determined the NATO alliance is.

Michael Howard goads him with a long list of hard questions and the accusation of incompetence and lack of strategy and tactics on NATO's part. The trouble is that Howard for once has good points and many of us share the same view.

Unfortunately, Robin rises to the bait and snaps and chivvies and snarls at Howard, accusing him of spending more time criticising the government than condemning Milošević.

This produces howls of outrage from Conservatives and just sullen support from our backbenchers.

Tory after Tory rises to have a go at Robin, saying that they have the right to ask hard questions and he mustn't disparage their carrying out of that parliamentary duty.

Robin had by now lost the House completely and had to appeal to raw partisan loyalty, which was offered grudgingly to him by his own backbenchers, but there was none of the sure-footed control of the despatch box for which he was once famous.

Howard twists the knife at the end by getting up and asking Robin to withdraw and apologise for his accusations that Howard hadn't condemned Milošević sufficiently.

Robin had to mumble an apology and Howard had, for once, won. The problem is that the Tories are actually desperate to see Cook and Blair stumble over the war as in America where the isolationist right who couldn't get Clinton over Monica are determined to get him over Milošević. The failure to deliver victories on the ground and the endless mistakes that NATO seems to make fuel the scepticism about the efficiency of the conduct of the war.

Thursday, 13 May 1999
At the reception in Aachen for Tony Blair's Charlemagne prize I chatted briefly to Tim Garton-Ash, who was very enthusiastic about the speech and the whole event. He quizzed me on the approach for the war and when I said I genuinely felt it had to be seen through to the end he grinned in agreement. He had just been in Macedonia and said that the army officers he had spoken to there were doing a superbly competent job and were ready to go into Kosovo if ordered. The two of us chatted to Edward Heath who was completely of the opposite opinion:

"It's no good this war. We shouldn't have got into it. We should get out of it as soon as possible."

Tim said, "Even if it means making peace with Milošević and scuttling?"

Ted replied with a grunt. "Yes. The Americans are no good. The Russians will have to do all this for us. But it can't go on. It simply can't go on."

What a fat old defeatist he is. I wonder how he squares all this with his anti-appeasement origins in politics in the late 1930s. Of course, he hates the Americans more than anything else and anything they are involved in he is against.

Tuesday, 18 May 1999
There is a bit of a discussion on Kosovo as there will be a debate on the war directly after Foreign Office questions. One of the officials

refers to a request faxed in by Alastair Campbell for Robin to write an article. "What's it all about?" he asks.

"Don't worry, Secretary of State," says Sherard Cowper Coles, his Private Secretary, "It's complete gibberish and I'll deal with it".

I have never heard Campbell referred to in that way by a senior official and it is quite cheery.

Wednesday 19 May 1999
Robin let slip one or two nuggets of information I hadn't heard before. The first being that almost irrespective of the outcome of the war there is going to be a huge problem of winter refugees. Thus, we create our own Gaza Strip in the Balkans. The second point was that "we are going through some dark days" which was a reference to all this morning's papers saying that the German Chancellor, Schröder, has snubbed Cook and Blair by saying the ground forces are "unthinkable". This doesn't quite stack up as none of the German papers quote him using that word "unthinkable".

Later I investigate this and get the transcript of Schröder's press conference in Bari where he was yesterday with Massimo D'Alema. He never used the word "unthinkable" at all. All he said is that "for Germany, the use of ground troops is not being considered or is not an option". I telephone Charles Reiss, the Evening Standard *political editor who first used the word "unthinkable" in his front-page splash yesterday. He tells me he got it from Reuters. I phone the Reuters' correspondent in Rome and he reads me back his notebook, in which he has written back "impencible". He tells me he doesn't speak German and so it was the Italian interpreter who had ratcheted up Schröder's more cautious statement into a crunchy one-word headline – "unthinkable". I write a quick note on this and call up David Leigh at* The Guardian, *but, of course, he is completely uninterested. How predictable* The Guardian *is.*

Sunday, 23 May 1999
The war itself is continuing its miserable course. Endless bombing, which, however precise, must be doing immense damage to this country and a stubborn refusal by Milošević to accept the bottom line of ending his state-sanctioned persecution of the Kosovans. The allies are at sixes and sevens over sending in ground troops but even if they are committed it is not a guaranteed outcome. Blair has to win this and in a sense has positioned himself so that if the allies win cleanly then as the most forthright leader, he will emerge with credit; if, on the other hand, there is a fudged up compromise then he will have been let down by his wimpish allies across the Atlantic or Channel. Clinton, too, has to win it to go down in history as a president who had retrieved some honour for America except that he is creating no moral fervour over there.

Friday, 4 June 1999
It really does look as if the Kosovo war might be over. The Yugoslav Parliament has agreed to accept the NATO peace offer. I won't be convinced until there are democratic troops in Kosovo.

Tuesday, 8 June 1999
I went to my office and then to the House for Blair's statement on Kosovo. It was measured and completely untriumphant. There were no real cheers from our side and the Tories only got going about Europe as Blair had to cover the well nigh irrelevant European Council meeting in Cologne last week. He dealt with aggressive questions from Tony Benn firmly and I think emerged in the House as he has in the country, as a real quality leader. He again got passionate about Europe and warned Hague that his anti-European politics might bring short-term tactical advantage, but were going to do damage in the medium and long term. I hope that is true and certainly Blair sounded as if he meant it.

Thursday, 17 June 1999
There is a debate on Kosovo today.

The Chamber was thin, very thin. Robin made a good combative speech. He is much more relaxed and self-confident. I thought he would miss Michael Howard as his opponent but although Howard cranked him up there was always that lurking danger that he might land an effective punch. John Maples, Howard's replacement as shadow foreign secretary, is much weaker. He effects an air of studied reasonableness and has a nice speaking voice. Listening to him is a bit like listening to John Major. It's fluent, coherent, every idea in its place, but no idea with any weight or punch.

Cookie has a go at the SNP and a turn at those who criticized the government's handling of the war in the "dark days", when the news about NATO bombing mistakes filled the front pages.

I think that as good as Robin has been in helping keep all the different bits of the coalition together, there is some puffing up in all of this. History will record a sub-colonial military sortie to put an unruly tribal chief back in his place. We have been lobbing our shells into the heart of darkness and finally the wicked head of the Serb tribe realized he couldn't take on the empire any longer and slunk back to his mountain fastness. Robin is putting this two-month campaign on a par with the Second World War or other huge global conflicts. Nonetheless, it is a competent speech and goes down well.

I drift in and out for the rest. There is some windy bombast from the "told you so" brigade and no little jeering and self-indulgence by those who have supported the conflict. Alice Mahon is brave and stands up to defend her position that it was all a ghastly mistake and the Serbs are equal victims to the Kosovan Albanians. Really, with all the news coming out of the atrocities, torture chambers, mass graves, and other evidence that the Serbs are not just being beastly but inhumanely brutal and murderous I think she might have had just a little more discretion. But she is *a plucky Yorkshire girl and battles on against wind and tide and I admire her for it.*

These extracts from my journal are to give a flavour of how the Kosovan war was seen from the perspective of the House of Commons. Conservatives like Sir Malcolm Rifkind and Norman Lamont, and nationalists like Alex Salmond all opposed the military force used to liberate Kosovo. As 500,000 Kosovan refugees returned home the opposition of these right-wingers seemed misplaced. The returning Kosovans were not tender with Serbs. While Milošević and the string-pullers of Serb hate against Kosovans remained in safety in Belgrade, there were acts of brutality inside Kosovo itself. The Kosovan editor and publisher, Veton Surroi, appealed to the readers of his paper, *Koha Ditore*, to accept responsibility for Kosovan crimes unleashed after NATO forces took control of the country.

> In the past month an old woman has been beaten to death in her bath; a two-year old boy has been wounded and his mother shot dead; two youths have been killed with a grenade launcher.
>
> I know how Kosovo's remaining Serbs, and indeed Roma feel, because I along with nearly 2 million Albanians, was in exactly the same situation only two and a half months ago. I recognize their fear...I know the obvious excuse, namely that we have been through a barbaric war in which Serbs were responsible for heinous crimes and in which the intensity of violence has generated a desire for vengeance among many Albanians. This however is no justification.

Surroi described such ethnic hate and violence against Kosovan Serbs as "fascist... It was against these very same attitudes that the people of Kosovo stood up and fought, at first peacefully, and then with arms during the past ten years. The treatment of Kosovo's Serbs bring shame on all Kosovo Albanians ...from having been the victims of Europe's worst end-of-century persecution, we are ourselves becoming persecutors and have allowed the spectre of fascism to reappear."

Surroi's brave warning and appeal found little echo at the time. A spirit of revenge similar to the savage *épuration* of extra-judicial killings and violence that the French Resistance wreaked upon opponents in the weeks after the liberation of France in 1944 took hold in Kosovo. However Surroi was wrong to think this would last. As the 21st century opened the politics of nationalist hate were stronger in Belgrade than in Pristina. He has continued to write with courage and clear-sightedness about his country. At some stage a process of truth, reconciliation and healing will be needed. And Kosovans should accept that cruel and unacceptable acts of hate and vengeful violence against Serbs did take place in the months after the liberation of Kosovo in 1999.

On the ground in Kosovo itself there was an energetic effort to try and show how the international community of democracies could not just win a war but help build a country. More than a decade later this task is not finished. Belgrade and Moscow were not able to maintain Serb occupation and control of Kosovo. But with a patient determination to make life as awkward for the Kosovan people as possible the Serbs and Russians have fought a long battle to prevent Kosovo from accepting its due if modest place in the world community of nations.

7

Minister for the Balkans

The United Nations moved quickly to take over the administration of Kosovo. The UN Interim Administration Mission
in Kosovo – or UNMIK as it became known – was bolstered by
the NATO military force, KFOR, in charge of security: KFOR
was answerable to NATO not UNMIK. The UN Secretary
General also appointed a Special Representative. But his powers
were limited.

There is still a UN Special Representative – the Italian diplomat, Lamberto Zannier. UNMIK still exists. What was put
together in the excitement of Milošević agreeing to withdraw
from Kosovo in 1999 has turned by 2011 into a testament to the
inability of the UN to find a solution to its superfluous presence
in Kosovo. As long as Russia remains hostile to a peace settlement based on the will of the Kosovan nation this unsatisfac-
tory state of affairs will continue.

As the London School of Economics's Spyros Economides
has written, "The inherent paradox in the United Nations' (UN)
intervention is that it did not occur until after a ceasefire has
been reached on the ground." With hindsight we can see that
the drafters of the UN Resolution 1244 left too many questions
unanswered. As the world relaxed in the summer of 1999 with
the feeling that the decade-long Balkan wars might finally be
over no one noticed the sloppy wording. No one appeared to

have read David Hume in his *Treatise of Human Nature*: "There is no quality in human nature which causes more fatal errors in our conduct than that which leads us to prefer whatever is present to the distant and remote."

UN resolutions are wordy documents in which all the different power-brokers in the world seek to defend their positions. Most of the Resolution deals with removing the Serb military forces, disarming the Kosovan Liberation Army, and setting out UNMIK's duties and legal authority. But the worm in the bud of Resolution 1244 came in the middle of the text. The key clauses were 10 and 11 which said the UN:

> "Authorizes the Secretary-General, with the assistance of relevant international organizations, to establish an international civil presence in Kosovo in order to provide an interim administration for Kosovo *under which the people of Kosovo can enjoy substantial autonomy within the Federal Republic of Yugoslavia* [emphasis mine], and which will provide transitional administration while establishing and overseeing the development of provisional democratic self-governing institutions to ensure conditions for a peaceful and normal life for all inhabitants of Kosovo."

No one paid much attention to these few words. What they amounted to was Belgrade being given diplomatic victory after the defeat of its military efforts to maintain its policy of oppressing and subjugating the Kosovan nation and people. Kosovo had enjoyed a degree of autonomy within Yugoslavia between 1945 and Milošević's appeal to Serb nationalism in 1987. The Kosovans no longer wanted to be subject to Belgrade's rule. Yugoslavia had been declared dissolved in 1992. Yet here was the UN restoring – as the language of Resolution 1244 appeared to argue – Kosovo as simply part of Serbia. This textual blunder left the door open to those who still argue today that Kosovo is part of Serbia. In a letter sent to Ban Ki-moon, the UN Secretary General, and circulated at the United Nations in August 2011, Vuk Jeremić, Serbia's Minister of Foreign Affairs described the government of Kosovo as "the ethnic-Albanian secessionist leadership" who preside over "an illegitimate regime". Like the Bourbons it would appear that some in Belgrade have learnt nothing and forgotten nothing. But this extraordinary language about the democratically-elected government of a neighbouring country could only be used in 2011 because in 1999 the clever diplomats at the UN did not think through the consequences of the words they wrote. These words left Kosovo in limbo in terms of its status once the Serbian soldiers and paramilitaries had been forced to leave the country they had first invaded and colonized in 1912.

The first of these UN Secretary General's Special Representatives (UNSGSR) was the dynamic figure of Bernard Kouchner from France. A left-wing doctor who came out of the 1968 movement to become a full-time political internationalist, Kouchner regularly topped polls as France's most popular political figure. He had been minister for overseas aid under François Mitterrand and then health minister. His wife Christine Ockrent was France's most-admired television news show host, who managed on the side to write serious books of biography and political history. Kouchner had founded *Médicins sans Frontières* – the legendary French doctors, the 20th century equivalent of the Red Cross – and had a legion of admirers in global politics.

The UN Secretary General, Kofi Annan, phoned Kouchner and asked him to go to Pristina as his special representative, in effect, the international community's pro-consul in Kosovo. Kouchner and all subsequent UN special representatives had to operate under the UN resolution, No 1244, which went on in Clause 11 to define UNMIK's role as

(a) Promoting the establishment, *pending a final settlement*, of substantial autonomy and self-government in Kosovo;

(b) Performing basic civilian administrative functions where and as long as required;

(c) Organizing and overseeing the development of provisional institutions for democratic and autonomous self-government *pending a political settlement*, including the holding of elections;

(d) Transferring, as these institutions are established, its administrative responsibilities while overseeing and supporting the consolidation of Kosovo's local provisional institutions and other peace-building activities;

(e) *Facilitating a political process designed to determine Kosovo's future status."* [emphasis mine]

Again the words are vitally important and lie at the root of the continuing and tragic stalemate of the Western Balkans. Kosovo had waited for decades to become a small, modest, poor – to begin with – Balkan nation. It had tried the pacifist tactics of Rugova. It then turned to a brief foray into national liberation armed resistance. The democratic world's military power had forced Milošević to retreat. But the democratic world's UN diplomats had made the historic error of failing to turn the end of the conflict into the birth of a Kosovan nation-state under international supervision. The weasel words about "future status" and "pending a final" or "political settlement" allowed Belgrade and, behind Belgrade, Russia, all the diplomatic room for manoeuvre to delay and thwart the hopes of June 1999 that, finally, the people of Kosovo could emerge into the daylight of nationhood.

In his book (*Les guerriers de la paix* (The Warriors of Peace)) about his time in Kosovo, Kouchner skates over this fundamental problem. He describes his efforts to get Albanians and Serbs, including the frightened priests in charge of Serb churches and monasteries, to cooperate. Kouchner received visits from the government leaders who had prosecuted the war. Tony Blair was received rapturously and plans were made to erect a statue to Bill Clinton, which still stands on Pristina's main street.

Kouchner had to oversee a diverse group of UN officials from different countries and cultures. For some, it was just a job with good allowances. UNMIK was accused of facilitating and organising the trafficking of sex slaves from Moldova and Bulgaria. In a Kosovo where some men – both Albanian and Serb – took the abuse of prostituted women and girls for granted, the treatment of women was appalling. But the UNMIK boss had little power to hire and fire. Far from being an omnipotent pro-consul, he got trapped in the swamp of UN protocols and rules, as well as a great deal of sympathy from UN officials who disliked the West and sympathised with the continuing obduracy of the Serbs.

He stayed for less than two years and a succession of UN Special Representatives followed. They all came with energy and determination. They left disappointed men. One of Kouchner's successors, the highly respected Norwegian international diplomatist, Kai Eide, reported in 2005 that UNMIK had failed in its task: "The current economic situation remains bleak [...] respect for rule of law is inadequately entrenched and the mechanisms to enforce are not sufficiently developed [...] with regard to the foundations of a multiethnic society, the situation is grim."

In their book *Peace at Any Price. How the World Failed Kosovo*, published in 2006, Iain King and Whit Mason – who worked for UNMIK – expose its many failings. Both men are dedicated internationalists and competent professionals. But the overall problem lay not with the nature of UNMIK, the multitude of agencies all refusing to cooperate, or the sordidly casual and cynical behaviour of some international officials. The root cause of the problem was the failure to allow the emergence of a Kosovan state, able to exercise authority on the basis of a constitutional and elected authority over its own territory.

As King and Whitman argue, security must have top priority before democracy and "a mission must be prepared to assert its authority from day one". KFOR and UNMIK failed to take control of Mitrovica, and the region of Kosovo north of the Ibar river in the immediate aftermath of the retreat of the Serb army. Attention focused on the sudden arrival of Russian troops at Pristina airport. They were quickly surrounded by NATO troops and found they could not be supplied. The Russian slunk home and NATO generals congratulated themselves on their handling of the stand-off.

Theirs was a tactical victory. The strategic mistake of political leaders was the failure to ensure that the writ and authority of KFOR and the UN was established all over Kosovo. As a result, the Mitrovica triangle became a mafia training centre thanks to the absence of law and the crude encouragement by Belgrade of Serb separatism. Violence and unchecked criminality was seen to pay off. Tackling this and imposing security all over Kosovo should have had priority. But with every decision having to be referred back to the UN headquarters in New York and with the KFOR troops micro-managed by the defence ministries of each contingent's home nation, this was easier said than done.

Between 2001 and 2005, I was responsible on behalf of the British government for our policy in the Balkans. My contemporaneous journal notes provide an insight into the frustrations and difficulties of finding peace in Kosovo. I was appointed in June 2001 and, as soon as I could, I went to the region.

Wednesday, 18 July 2001
Out on an early plane to Paris and then on to Belgrade. A very bright energetic ambassador, full of ideas and clever words, who lives in a splendid residence set out a bit like Lord Levy's house in a Reader's Digest 1960 ranch style. He took me to see a small

committee of Serbian people whose relatives had disappeared or gone missing in Kosovo. Awful heart-breaking stories and the sense of victimhood reeked everywhere. I offered maximum sympathy and said nice words but told them they had to turn the corner and participate in democratic politics. They didn't like that. They want their Kosovo back. They want the Albanians punished. Quite clearly this whole region will either become a Gaza Strip or West Bank or it will become like Cyprus after 1974 where the bitterness and anger and sense of dispossession remains but people just get on with their lives. Belgrade is obviously a great European city. Everywhere there was strength and life and the potential to make it one of the leading capital cities of a modern Europe if only they would all seize the opportunity. I went to the B92 radio and TV station. This was the great democratic opposition to Milošević and it's good to honour these people.

My ministerial duties took me to Latin America, Asia and to the United States. In both Washington and at the United Nations in New York I had a sense of American and UN policy-makers feeling that Kosovo was mission accomplished. An election had been held and Ibrahim Rugova had been chosen as president, leaving the field of executive government to the KLA-linked PDK party. A surgeon, Bajram Rexhepi, was installed as prime minister. But these grand titles counted for little as effective power lay with the international institutions.

In Washington I met the usual competent State Department officials but, politically, the Balkans was Clinton's foreign policy region. The new George W. Bush administration knew it was important to stay there. I insisted that only the Stars and Stripes flying off US jeeps and armoured personnel carriers would be strong enough as a symbol to both reassure the Kosovans that the Serbs were not about to return and convey a message to any revengeful Kosovar Albanians that Western values were now those expected to be upheld.

Periodically, there were reports that the overstretched US military might pull out of Kosovo and close down their big Camp Bondsteel base. To her credit, the then Secretary of State, Condoleeza Rice, insisted that the US would maintain a presence, but the attack on New York on 9/11 changed the entire focus of US and Western foreign policy. Kosovo slipped way down the agenda. The geo-political energy that had been deployed to stop Milošević in 1999 was now channeled into what George W. Bush called the "War on Terror".

Europe, which had been united under social democratic leadership in 1999, now became divided. The German Chancellor Gerhard Schröder and his Foreign Minister, Joschka Fischer – from the Green Party – had bravely changed the German constitution to allow German soldiers to serve outside the narrow confines of defending German territory as part of NATO. German soldiers would now be like other European military, able to don a UN blue helmet and use weapons of war as part of a NATO, UN or EU mission.

The Bundestag maintained a tighter parliamentary control than in other democracies, but the decisive break with the post-war agreement that limited German military operations to national self-defence had been achieved. Indeed, it had been a German officer leading his men who had first crossed the border from Macedonia into Kosovo when the NATO ground operation began. With a coolly brave insouciance, he walked up to the Serb officer and gently pushed his weapon to one side. It was a symbolic movement that announced the end of Serb military domination in Kosovo.

In September 2002, Schröder had to fight a difficult election. German public opinion, on the Catholic right as much as on the secular left, was openly hostile to US policy in Iraq. Schröder had to come out full-square against the use of force to uphold UN resolutions in Iraq unless sanctioned by a UN resolution. This policy, in effect, meant handing over the decision to the

neo-authoritarian Vladimir Putin and the Communist polit-
buro in China. France's Jacques Chirac, who now had control
of the National Assembly and the French government, threw in
his lot with Schröder. As a result, Europe was fatally split in half
on the issue of solidarity with Washington. This Euro-Atlantic
turmoil shoved Kosovo onto the back burner.

Meanwhile, Milošević had been arrested in March 2001 on
suspicion of corruption, abuse of power and embezzlement.
The Serbs finally lost patience with the man who had brought
so much hurt and harm to Serbia. As protests in Belgrade gathered in strength, the Serb military and security elites called
time on Milošević. An MI6 plane was sent down to Belgrade
and, before the world was fully aware of his arrest and rendi-
tion, the Serb leader was in The Hague where he died in 2006
waiting for the verdict on his charges of war crimes. While the
Serb military establishment and the ruling elites in Belgrade
were willing to get rid of Milošević, they were not prepared to
make a final peace in Kosovo.

At the end of the 19th century the British prime minister,
Lord Salisbury, told Parliament that he "would no more give
democracy to the Irish than to the Hottentot." This racist con-
descension from a superior power towards the subordinate
nation it believes is incapable of running its own affairs is all too
common throughout colonialist history. For Serbia, Kosovo had
always been a kind of colony, inhabited by an inferior people.
The Lord Salisburies of Belgrade were much in evidence after
Milošević's departure. The situation in Kosovo was not going
well either.

Monday, 25 February 2002
*To Gatwick to fly to Pristina: where I meet politicians who simply
won't accept any responsibility to govern at all. The National
Assembly was elected last November but no one has an absolute
majority and the different Albanian parties are manoeuvring to*

block each other. The clear winner is Ibrahim Rugova, the soft, slight, intellectual who maintained the identity and sense of independence of Kosovo during the worst of the Milošević years. It was the first time I met him. He was wearing the scarf from the district in which he was born, which has become his trademark, and was in a beautifully cut suit. We spoke in French to keep the conversation flowing without an interpreter. Tough on the local officials and David (my private secretary) but f*** it, they are paid to learn languages. He had beautiful central European intellectual's hands with perfect oval nails. I told him that modern Europe didn't like secession and instead believed in regional and national autonomy without independent statehood. He wasn't interested in my little sermon.

The two other men were leaders of the KLA and both have got serious blood on their hands. Not mass slaughter bloodshed in the style of a Serb or Croat killer, just the murder here and there of fellow Albanians they accused of collaborating or their enemies of one sort or another. One, Thachi, was the darling of Madeleine Albright, at their Rambouillet negotiations. The other gave me another copy of his biography with himself strutting in camouflage uniform on the back. Do they realize the war is now three years in the past? It's like being in France in 1948 and resistance chieftains still wanting to be recognized for what they did then rather than dealing seriously with the politics of now. But, between them and the frightened little Serbs who don't want to get involved in Albanian Kosovan politics, they have enough votes to stop Rugova being named president. Each wants to be the Prime Minister but the UN bosses who actually run Kosovo won't allow someone who could be arrested on war crimes or just ordinary crime charges to become PM. A nice little Balkan stand-off.

I also talked to Michael Steiner, who was Gerhard Schröder's chief international fixer. He is now the pro-consul of Kosovo. He has shining white teeth and looks like Jack Nicholson as the Joker in Batman. He has come in with lots of enthusiasm and wants to fix a government but is slowly realising that Pristina politics are a complete quicksand. If he is not careful he will be up to his ankles, then his knees and goodbye. I wish him well. At least he does things with enthusiasm and authority, so he may carry something off, but this place is not susceptible to normal Western political fixing.

Tuesday, 26 February 2002

Today was for the military and we met General Valentin, the dapper wiry white-haired French General who runs KFOR. He had already been out for his "footing" (morning run). His chief of staff was a fat, paunch-bellied British brigadier from the Royal Artillery. But of course they got on fine: brisk, to the purpose and quite keen to reduce the number of troops in KFOR but not to merge them with the Bosnian force, SFOR. I asked why the French soldiers in Bosnia had failed to arrest Karadžić. General Valentin was diplomatic but his political adviser, a young little thug from Matignon, got very bristly and said, "How can we do this? He is surrounded by armed men. It would need 500 soldiers to mount an operation." "Et alors?" I asked. There was no answer, only grumpiness as the French could not even face being questioned. I am really fed up with the equivocation from both the French and the Americans and their joint failure to take real action on these mass murderers.

The British troops were all commanded by a Brigadier Buffy who was very much a cavalry man and public school. But he said he admired the calm professionalism of our men overseas.

I went into an odd little police operation with people seconded from different British police units drawing up some kind of map of criminals in Kosovo. Looking at their work I was tempted to say that a good crime editor could do all this in a couple of days, but they all were sitting around in a little portacabin opposite, beavering away and feeling good. I hope it leads on to arrests and convictions but I have doubts.

Pristina looked busier with traffic jams everywhere. The streets were still poor and there was nothing new in the shops. I did an aggressive press conference calling on the Kosovan politicians to accept their responsibilities and form a government. I am everywhere in newspapers and on the television but it is just shouting into the wind.

In London I spent time giving evidence to Parliamentary Committees and answering questions about the Balkans. Tony Blair had decided to send Paddy Ashdown to Sarajevo to try and put some momentum in the stalemate between the Serbs in Bosnia and their Bosniak and Croat fellow-citizens. Like Bernard Kouchner, Ashdown went to the Balkans full of energy, ideas and hope. Bosnia today is still a mess.

Thursday, 25 April 2002
An interesting discussion on Kosovo today. Jack Straw (Robin Cook's successor as Foreign Secretary) has brought together all the top officials and we go round the houses on what to do. The Ministry of Defence has made clear it wants to get out of either Bosnia or Kosovo. In its own paper it recommends pulling out of Kosovo and concentrating all our troops in Bosnia. I protest that this is just the comfort factor at play. The army has loads of barracks in Bosnia and has been going there for nearly ten years. They don't do much. But it's an easy pair of shoes to wear as a policy choice. In Kosovo we have a strategic interest because that is a fault line with Macedonia, with Albania, with Greece. It's also Blair's war and to scuttle in Kosovo would look odd. But there is the Paddy (Ashdown) factor. Paddy called me up and said that he would be very opposed to having all British troops taken away in Bosnia just at the moment when he was advising there. I agreed with him but a choice has to be made. I still think Kosovo is where we should be present.

Charles Crawford, the sharp but rather cocky ambassador in Belgrade, says that we should stay in Bosnia and that Kosovo should be persuaded to be in a loose federation with Serbia and Montenegro. I think this is an unlikely idea and said, "Imagine being here ten years ago. The Foreign Secretary and his key advisers would have been saying that at all costs we must hold Yugoslavia together. It was a complete waste of policy and resources. At times you have to let go. If Kosovo is going to go independent let's go with reality and stop pretending otherwise even if it means swallowing one or two of our existing statements". Backwards and forwards went the argument. At the end Jack said, "Well what are we gonna do?" I said, "Let's have a vote. Let's just see a show of hands to see who's in favour of the Kosovo options or who's for putting all our troops into Bosnia and leaving Kosovo". The officials looked horrified. Everyone was nervous but Jack just went with the idea so I grabbed a couple of sheets of paper and tore them up into tiny slips and handed them round to the fifteen or so people around this table. "Write 'K' or 'B'," I said and gathered in all the papers. It was ten votes in favour of Kosovo and five for Bosnia. Thus, British foreign policy is made.

I met Kosovan and Serb political leaders in London and Brussels. Croatia's failure to find and surrender Ante Gotovina – the indicted former soldier from the French Foreign Legion who had awarded himself the rank of "General" in Tudjman's war of ethnic cleansing in Croatia – was a major obstacle to Croatia's beginning along the road to EU membership. I went to Zagreb to both support Croatia's EU ambitions, despite the increasing hostility to the European Union being whipped up in London, and to insist Gotovina had to be found and sent to The Hague. When I could, I travelled to the West Balkans to see for myself what was going on.

Tuesday, 2 July 2002
A long, tiring but satisfying day. Breakfast with Dr Kovic who is in charge of Serbian relations with Kosovo. He was glum and

miserable and said it was all going badly. Basically, they still see Kosovo as a Serbian province and can't bear the fact that Kosovan Albanians are doing to them what they did to the Albanians in the 1980s and 1990s. It is frankly a nightmare. Part of me wants just a repartition and to let the Serbs have the chunk of Kosovo where they have a lot of their population. But this could lead to further pressure on all the Serbs elsewhere in Kosovo to flee and make the point of the military intervention null and void.

The highly polite and calmly spoken President Koštunica, whose moderate and modest style hides a raving Serb national-ist, was as usual polite as he told me that English MPs supported Serbia entering the Council of Europe. I will talk to Terry Davis about this but I expect they have sold the pass.

Then onto the Defence Minister. He was surrounded by lieu-tenant generals and major generals but they only had two rows of medal ribbons, which seemed quite right because the only fight-ing and killing they had done was against their own people. But I still don't know where all the medals that British and American generals wear come from, given that we don't do wars these days.

The Defence Minister, I notice, is unable to mention the name of Mladić or Karadžić. So I prompt him and he immediately comes back with the remark that they are not on Serbian terri-tory. It is complete bullshit and an excuse.

General Krga comes in to support his minister but is more emollient: "I appreciate the desire to sort out the question of war criminals. We are seriously interested in solving this. We have to act in compliance with International Law. No one wearing the uniform VJ," and as he mentions his army he touches his own lapel, "has committed any crimes. The VJ protects no one and certainly not Mladić and Karadžić."

It was a dialogue of the deaf. I had made my points and it was time to move on.

Back in London it was difficult to get much attention for

Kosovo as all the focus was on the Iraq crisis.

Tuesday, 15 October 2002
*I saw the most extraordinary letter from Claire Short (the Over-
seas Aid and Development minister) today. It was addressed to
Blair and was her impression of Serbia and Kosovo. On Serbia
everything was going extremely well, reforms were in hand, the
leadership was set fair for Europe and there were no problems. In
Kosovo, by contrast, the United Nations operation was a disaster
and all power should be handed over to the Kosovan Albanians
as soon as possible to get things moving. It was naïve gibberish. I
began scribbling out an angry reply but James Bevan, the official
who deals with the Balkans and who is very bright said, "Oh,
Claire sends one of these letters every fortnight. We know Blair
take no notice of them. Maybe we can turn it to our advantage
and get her to agree to sit on a Cabinet Committee that could
examine the Balkan problem and maybe she should put some
DfID money into helping people both in Kosovo and Serbia."*

The Iraq invasion in March 2003 further sidelined Kosovo.
That month saw the assassination of the pro-West Serb prime
minister Zoran Djindjić. A hitman linked to the Serb security
forces and Belgrade criminal networks killed him as both the
state intelligence services and the Serb Mafiosi were worried at
Djindjić's reforms aimed at reducing their power and influence.
Fluent in German and English, Djindjić had been a resolute
opponent of Milošević. But he was unable to change the political culture of his nation before his murder.

Sunday, 6 April 2003
*As soon as I arrive there I am taken to the grave of Zoran Djindjić
– the assassinated Serbian leader. I place a wreath on his grave
and stand in solemn silence. He was a reformist, a clever man
and very European with some allegations of dodgy links here and*

there and a willingness to cut corners that perhaps was not a manifestation of the highest level of political propriety. I gave a short interview to B92, the Liberal TV station, and then it's off to see an interior minister. He says that 9,000 people had been taken in for questioning after the assassination and 2,600 had been arrested or charged. The notorious Red Berets outfit has been disbanded. More people would go up to the International Criminal Tribunal in The Hague. The statistics are all good and roll out with some punch. But have they simply rounded up the usual suspects or dug up an old "B" list of people that the new government would want to arrest and intimidate in any case? I simply don't know enough internal Serb politics to get a feel, but undoubtedly some of the rotten flesh left over from the Milošević era is being slashed away and that has to be a good sign.

Back for a dinner at the Embassy with the ever ebullient Charles Crawford, one of the most whizzing catherine wheels of a politically acute ambassador that we have, putting together an impressive number of political leaders. All spoke English, just about, so we were able to round table talk in an effective way.

They were all quite bullish and confident, though once the state of emergency was over, it would be back to the dreary field of economics and, unless there was better news in terms of credits from the IMF or the EU or the International Donors, then the inevitable social explosions would devour Serbia. They were also all very bad on Kosovo. There was a good liberal social democratic type of man called Korac who said that as a Serb politician he had to represent the Serbs in Kosovo. I told him that as an English politician I didn't feel I had to represent the interests of Ulster Unionists or Catholic Nationalists in Northern Ireland. They had their own spokesman and that to offer to represent their interests was dangerous politics. He didn't like my comment and no doubt I was being pushy as an outsider but until Belgrade finds ways of letting go of Kosovo there will be no resolution of the Serbian question.

The Serbs feel victims of a world conspiracy to do them down.

They have lost the country they used to run – Yugoslavia – the economic status they had; the right to travel without visas anywhere in Europe; a good deal of their standard of living, and it is very hard to give up one of the last expressions of Serb identity, namely their hold and their cultural and historical interests in Kosovo. Yet they will have to come to terms with that before Serbia will ever come back to life again.

Monday, 7 April 2003

We fly in a small twin propeller plane to Kosovo. Because the Serbs do not allow a direct flight to Pristina we have to go all the way down to Skopje in Macedonia and then turn back to land in Pristina. It is all absolutely pathetic and shows the mean mindedness and pettiness of the Belgrade authorities.

I got another lump of Kosovo crystal from President Rugova to give to the Prime Minister back home. Rugova receives me in his office, which has got heavy padded plastic furniture. He still wears his scarf tucked into his pullover – he is right to wear one as it is jolly cold and there have been snow flurries in the air – and goes on and on about the need for Kosovo to have its own independence. In my mind I half agree. The country will go nowhere unless it knows what it is. But, as with the sense of victimhood in Belgrade, there is a permanent sense of whining in Pristina that someone else is responsible for their misery rather than their own inability to make rules and stick to them. The Prime Minister, whom I see next, is a lot better and clearer but we are now four years after the conflict and nobody knows who really runs or governs Kosovo. Pristina itself seems more bustling than a year ago or when I first visited two years ago. It is good to come here just see things for myself and get the feel of what is going on.

A party at one of the British staff's house is heaving. There are two or three top Serb politicians amongst a mainly Kosovo and international crowd. I chat to one very intelligent lawyer from Mitrovica. He basically wants a cantonisation of the country with distinct Serb enclaves that are ruled 100 per cent by Serbs for Serbs and the rest of Kosovo can go hang.

I meet a fat little chief of police. A twinkling bald Friar Tuck figure in his brand new uniform which already has one medal ribbon in it. I dare not ask him what he won it for. He insists that Serbs and Kosovan police officers are patrolling together but someone tells me later that he has got very strong links to business. Enough said.

Dinner with a couple of journalists and Hashim Thaçi, the handsome Kosovan politician, who was a spokesman for the Liberation Army at the talks of Rambouillet in 1999. He seems as always a smart and articulate fellow. Scarlett McGuire, who comes out from the Westminster Foundation of Democracy to try and teach these guys some politics, is obviously completely in love with him. And he says good things like not discussing independence for three years, which makes a lot of sense. And yet at some stage he was linked to some bad people who did bad things and as a result can't get a visa to go to different countries in Europe. I will need to check into this and just see whether he is someone we should work with or whether his past puts him beyond the pale.

Tuesday, 8 April 2003

Staying in the best hotel in Pristina but it still doesn't have curtains that cover the windows so again I sleep badly.

Breakfast with a cool agreeable enthusiastic army officer, Brigadier Jonathan Shaw. He is off to be director of special forces a.k.a. the SAS and the people who go off and do funny things in funny places at funny times of the night. He says that he doesn't think British forces should be leaving Kosovo. "What?!" I say. It was the Defence Ministry that insisted the army pull out of Kosovo to go to Bosnia where they are much more comfortably installed and have got absolutely nothing to do. He insists that it was a Foreign Office decision. Well, as usual in government everyone blames someone else for a decision that is controversial but I am fairly sure in my own mind it was the MoD that wanted this.

Against this background, the specific decisions are taken by a host of officials without reference to a minister. If ordered to do something, like invade Iraq, Whitehall obeys orders. Even a Foreign Secretary, despite the grand title and size of his office with its red leather armchairs, finds he executes foreign policy decisions taken in Downing Street and conveyed to him by functionaries. Foreign ministers, after all, come and go. The head of the Foreign Office is not called the Permanent Under Secretary by accident. The Whitehall decision to move experienced British troops out of Kosovo, first to Bosnia and then to Iraq, removed key professional soldiers at a crucial moment. The delaying tactics in Belgrade and the focus of all global politics on Iraq left the Western Balkans without the external pressure, which appeared to be the only way to get movement.

In March 2004 there had been ugly riots in Kosovo after (false) reports of Serbs drowning Kosovan children. Thirty people had been killed and hundreds wounded after Kosovan Albanians attacked Serb villages and churches. KFOR had been slow to react. Different national contingents had varied weaponry but little experience of riot control. German soldiers refused to go out in the dark on orders from Berlin. Sadly the decision to remove British troops left a major gap in the ability of KFOR to contain the violence at an early stage. The 2004 riots again highlighted the lack of effective state authority in Kosovo, which the UN, NATO and EU agencies could not replace.

Tuesday, 20 April 2004
Down to Macedonia. On the plane this morning Misha Glenny has joined us. He, of course, knows everybody and everything in the region though is seen to have a slight bias towards the Slavs and the Serbs. We drive to Pristina through good mountain countryside. As internationals we can take a kind of bypass road at the frontier where the lorries queue up. This is where the troops

passed in 1999. I am here because five years later on not enough has moved.

I had asked to see Swiss soldiers but they are in the far north of Kosovo.

In fact I had had a wonderful two hours with an Irish unit – real tough professionals who had been on border patrols between Northern Ireland and the Republic and were calm and confident in crowd control and eliciting information. They showed me videos and still pictures of the riots on St. Patrick's Day a month ago and the day after the 18th March.

Koštunica, the Serb Prime Minister, made a provocative "Kosovo is ours" speech in his Parliament and, following some unexplained drowning in Mitrovica, Kosovo just exploded. Crowds of young boys, still at school, in college or without any employment or hope surged along the streets of Pristina and down the road to where the Irish troops were stationed, burning churches and Serb houses.

The Irish soldiers tried to form a line but the KFOR soldiers do not have the right to use water cannons or tear gas, and a number of the national units expressly forbid this. So there were few means of crowd control between holding up shields and using batons or actually opening fire. Norwegian and Swedish units did open fire with heavy machine guns and I shudder to think how close they might have come to a complete massacre.

The tension is awesome. I drove in an Irish jeep through a Serb village, Dubrotin. Sullen, dirty, shabby little houses of peasant existence. And before you know it the road has become the road of the Albanian village called Slovenje. There are still the burnt houses from 1998 and 1999 when the Serb militia and military attacked. We went on up to a cemetery on the hillside overlooking the sprawling village of about two thousand people. The little wooden markers of a Muslim cemetery showed the date of death of all the people there being the same year, 1999. The birth dates were 1912 or 1915 or my own birth, 1948. Just looking at where they had buried the men who were taken out and shot in cold blood by the Serbs helped to explain some of the level of hatred that exists between the two communities. Twenty-seven men were shot in cold blood but only eighteen bodies were actually discovered and nobody knows where the other nine are.

So with a heavy heart at this kind of misery we drove on into Pristina. Both the KFOR commander, a fairly useless German general with spiky crew cut hair, and the Finnish UN special representative, Harri Holkeri, filled me with despair. Neither had any energy or a sense of planning or even knowledge of what to do. Holkeri said he would be transferring economic competencies to the Kosovan provisional government. That would give them some status and let us see if they can then apply some decent standards and justify some transfer of power. But UNMIK, with their stupid white Toyota jeeps scurrying around the place, are now full of second-rate hacks who come and make as much money on per diems as they can (and worse) while they are there. No energy, no direction and a terrible sense of corruption and loss of purpose. [...] Seventy per cent of all the food consumed in Kosovo is imported, which is ridiculous as this is one of the richest and most fertile soils in Europe. The ground is full of minerals too but no one is here exploiting it. It just doesn't make sense.

Wednesday, 21 April 2004

I go and see President Rugova. As usual he had two big chunks of quartz to give me and I had prepared one from a Serb enclave to give back to him. But instead I had a better idea. Yesterday I went to see a Serb church, St. Nicholas, burnt down by the rioters on March 17–18. So I said to Rugova, "Why don't you come to the church with me and we can apologise for the crimes committed there by the Kosovan Albanians?" He looked at his adviser who nodded in agreement and said, "Why not?" We left the building having given the press a couple of minutes' notice and got into his big Rugova-mobile – a giant converted people carrier with two comfortable armchairs. We clambered around the burnt rubble of the church and he made all the right noises about this being a crime against European civilisation. It was an effective moment and the first time he had visited any one of the churches that his own people had burnt down so brutally a month ago. Gimmick politics perhaps, but also a bit of symbolism and some movement in this wretched country.

Up to Belgrade with the ludicrous business of having to touch down in Skopje because one cannot fly directly from Pristina to Belgrade.

It was the first complaint I made to the Serb Prime Minister, Koštunica, when I saw him. The meeting was anodyne. I didn't want to attack him even though his speech in the Serb Parliament at the beginning of March with its aggressive language on Kosovo undoubtedly helped spark the riots there. Instead we exchanged pleasantries. They are all terrified that a horrible right-wing pro-Milošević candidate will win the presidential election. All these silly countries have presidents and prime ministers for every mini part of them and I can't keep up with who is standing for what.

Dinner with the candidate, Boris Tadić, our guy, who is a very tall good looking democratic character. Beside him my old friend Goran Svilanovic. He was the urbane clever foreign minister but now he is out of a job. We have a nice dinner in an indifferent restaurant while he tries to work out what to do next. Such are Balkans politics. I have to say I don't trust any of them. I don't believe what they say. Perhaps they mean it when they say it but I just don't think they have any real capacity to deliver. I tell them all to work with the Kosovans to find a solution but they hate them with a deep, passionate and enduring hatred, as if twenty years ago you were telling Ian Paisley to sit down and compose his differences with Gerry Adams. It's going to go on bleeding in an unpleasant and disagreeable way.

Thursday, 22 April 2004

To the main mosque in Belgrade where a large beaming Hagrid of a man, the Mufti, greets me with great hugs and a mixture of garlic and tobacco on his breath. The mosque was attacked by Serb thugs in response to the riots in Kosovo. It took considerable time to restore order and the Serb authorities seem to allow their Muslim-hating thugs off the leash. The damage inside the mosque wasn't so bad but what horrified me was to go into the buildings behind it, including a library which had books that were two or three hundred years old. They lie on the floor burnt at the edges where the Serbs had thrown them into a fire. There is television and media everywhere and I tell people that you start burning books and you end up burning people. This is still a society too consumed by evil and hate without any leadership to take them into happier times. The Mufti insists that they want nothing to do with Wahibi or other extreme Islamist forms and I believe him. Even Nicolec, the candidate of Milošević for the presidency, is going around mosques trying to pick up votes. It is the absolute hate engendered in Kosovo that is the real problem.

Visits to the new Foreign Minister, Vuk Drašković, a black bearded enthusiast who was a major campaigner against Milošević in the 1990s. He says the right things about the need for Karadžić and Mladić to go to The Hague but doesn't give an inch on Kosovo. They still see this as defending their own people against evil Islamic terrorism.

President Marović is a bit better. I can talk to him in English, which he understands but he doesn't have enough to reply to me so we need an interpreter. I tell him that the speech by Koštunica in Parliament guaranteed a reaction from Kosovo because of its provocative terms. He is moderate in his tone and says he is going to visit Albania to try and build links with Tirana. But as always none of these presidents and prime ministers seem to be able to get out of their tramlines of existing thinking. I leave quite depressed. There doesn't seem to be any way out of this except *trying to ensure that the hates don't spill into violence. From Pristina comes the complaint that the visit to the Orthodox Church was not approved of by the local Orthodox Church and was a political stunt. Well of course it bloody was but what a stunt to get Rugova almost on his knees in one of the churches his people had destroyed apologising for what they had done.*

I was chancing my luck in making President Rugova come with me to the church and apologise for the criminal vandalism of his people. It played well on Serb television. But then Serbs became angry as I condemned the book-burning outside the Belgrade mosque and made the obvious comparison to the 1930s.

Most diplomacy is carried on behind closed doors. Ministers arrive via VIP entrances in airports, shake hands, have dinners, make a speech prepared by officials and leave. I wanted to be more present, more on the street. I also was gaining in confidence and knowledge.

At European Foreign Council meetings on Croatia, I simply vetoed any question of Croatia beginning EU accession talks until the Croatian war criminal, Ante Gotovina, was sent to The Hague. The Croatian president Stjepan Mesić was a reformer with a keen sense of social justice and a resolute opponent of the fascistic Croat leader, Tudjman. He made a special visit to the Labour Party conference to see Tony Blair to plead for British support for Croatia to begin EU talks. Blair's chief of staff, Jonathan Powell, conveyed the prime minister's view that it was a bit harsh to hold up Croatia "on account of one man."

I refused to drop my objections. Gotovina was a thug, but it was the entire state system of Croatia that was refusing to make the efforts to send him to The Hague. I stood my ground and Gotovina was discovered and sent for trial. In Belgrade the same points were being made about Karadžić and Mladić. Those two gentlemen were obstacles to Serbia moving EUwards. I was told that if Serb leaders moved to arrest Mladić there would be a national uprising and the democratic leaders would be overturned. Today, the same excuse is produced when Serb leaders are asked to recognize Kosovo. Sheltering behind the fear of the mob is not political leadership worthy of the name.

Monday, 25 October 2004

An early flight out to Belgrade where I go in and see all the main players – Tadić, Koštunica, the Foreign Minister, the President and so on. Once again, I am in despair. Yesterday there were elections in Kosovo but Koštunica ordered the Serbs living in Kosovo not to participate. Tadić, acting after I had called him and told him that democracy required the Serbs in Kosovo to vote, had issued an appeal in contrast to Koštunica's boycott demand. But although he spoke with the authority of the President of Serbia it fell on deaf ears and less than one percent of the Serbs actually cast a vote. As a result, the election in Kosovo showed the same people being sent back to the assembly in the same proportions as the last election three years ago. The Serbs won't play and still want to make the Kosovan Albanians pay for their liberation struggle.

It is complete impasse. My meetings are friendly enough and people go out of their way to listen to my points and to engage fully. But the feeling of the Serbs is so bitter and angry. Treading on the tail of the democrats are some pretty filthy ultra-nationalistic, extreme supporters of the Milošević era.

There is also very little movement on The Hague tribunal. I wonder if the next American president, whoever he is, will be able to show any energy in this area. I tell them that I have just come back from Cyprus where a failure to move has left the island divided for thirty years without proper political or economic hope. Serbia, I say again and again, cannot enter the EU until it has helped resolve both the Kosovo crisis and relationships, and delivered some of the indicted war criminals to The Hague tribunal. It is all a bit miserable.

Tuesday, 26 October 2004

I have the same feeling in Pristina. The usual round of discussions with the Albanian leaders with everyone camping on existing positions. For Rugova there is only one solution: Independence, now and immediately. I tell him the word to use is "Interdependence" and that Kosovo can stay locked in its present non-status for decades to come. Again, I remind them of Cyprus. The presence of the UN, international troops acting as a buffer, and communities just staring at each other across a wall of history and hate. But for the Kosovans it is a question of having liberated themselves from the hated rule of the Serbs, having organized a non-violent cultural civil society movement of resistance, and then an actual liberation war. They cannot understand why they can't become a full independent country. Maybe that is the only brutal way of getting out the forceps of Balkan history and seeing if we can give birth to something that can stand on its own feet. I am not sure that is the answer though.

In the time-honoured manner of British politics, just as a minister is getting to grips with his dossier, he is replaced. After the spring election in 2005, I had to leave office to allow Gordon Brown to promote one of his protegés. I did not mind as all ministerial office has to end. Moreover my relationship with Jack Straw – personally one of the kindest senior politicians I have worked with – was getting scratchy as my strong pro-European commitment jarred with the resurfacing of his long-held Eurosceptic views. Tony Blair asked me to become his personal envoy to Europe and I went off to visit European political leaders on his behalf. Yet the financing of this work later came to cause me problems as the British state refuses any money to envoys the prime minister nominates, unless they are on the Whitehall payroll.

I served as a delegate to the Council of Europe and the NATO parliamentary assembly and travelled to Pristina and other

Balkan capitals to keep in touch. British ambassadors and officials working with the international organization were always helpful and pleased, I think, that a former minister continued to take an interest. I visited Mitrovica with British army officers to stare across a cold war type check point which should have no place in modern Europe. I raised the issue of Kosovo in the Commons in debates and exchanges with ministers, including those who formed the new government after May 2010. Each time I went to Kosovo the country seemed more cheerful, more prosperous, and yet there remained the lack of what any people in Europe have a right to – their own nation and their own state.

8

Kosovo in the 21st Century – a Mixed Report

Kosovo enters the second decade of the 21st century in both a better and a worse state than its founding fathers would have thought. *Better* in that the country is free, and other than in the northern Mitrovica triangle, at peace. *Worse* because the continued Moscow-Belgrade blockage on Kosovo's acceptance as a normal European nation-state leaves the country unable to fulfil many of the roles of statehood.

Kosovo cannot join in normal regional or international regulatory bodies that determine frontier security or shared energy provision. Borders are closed. The main Serbia-Kosovo road crossing in northern Kosovo has no Kosovan frontier controls. International authorities do their best, but the triangle of territory north of the Ibar river is a happy hunting ground for criminality, as well as car, people and cigarette smuggling. When Kosovan customs officers did try to establish control of the border posts in July 2011, a Serb mob opened fire killing a Kosovan official.

Belgrade cynically encourages a zone of lawlessness in which Serb and Albanian mafia-style gangs cooperate. Sadly, Serbia's President Boris Tadić told Radio Free Europe in 2005 that Kosovo "could live only by smuggling drugs, people and weapons". His then foreign minister, Vuk Drašković, added

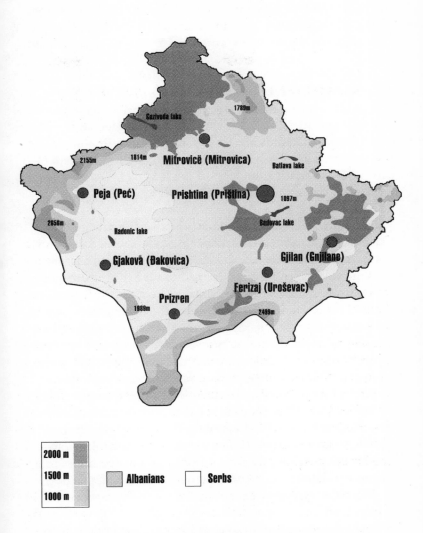

Serb communities are located in different regions of Kosovo just as there are Albanian communities in Serbia and Macedonia.

"An independent Kosovo would be economically isolated from Serbia and would not have any chance of surviving economically, so it would soon turn into a place of social riots and blood feuds."

It is the policy of Belgrade that creates the potential nightmare Serb leaders decry, even if their rhetoric is exaggerated. It is after all Serbians who protected the war criminals Radovan Karadžić and Ratko Mladić while Kosovan leaders accused of war crimes, like Ramush Haradinaj, had voluntarily gone to The Hague. Professor Henry Perrit, who worked for both Republican and Democratic presidents in the White House, offered an alternative vision in 2006 when he wrote

> One of the hallmarks of Kosovar society is the strong orientation toward entrepreneurship. Largely excluded from the formal economic system during 10 years repression by the Milošević regime, Kosovars learned to survive by setting up business ventures with little capital and access to infrastructure. Informal business networks exist throughout the region, into northern Europe and North America. Almost every family is in some kind of business, concentrating more on service and retail trade rather than manufacturing and processing. This pool of entrepreneurs offers significant opportunity to those who have the capacity to tie entrepreneurship to sources of adequate capital and modern business methods.
>
> Kosovars proved more willing than many expected to deposit their savings in the array of well-run banks established after the war. The major banking enterprises are tied to banking concerns in Western Europe, and use best practices in terms of internal auditing and conservative loan policies.

Certainly anyone who visits Pristina year on year has seen continuous improvements. What was a drab, shabby city in the aftermath of the Milošević years is now bustling with all the outward signs of modern city-life – traffic jams, endless internet cafés, and the best espresso coffee in the Balkans. Kosovo has slipped past landline telephones and 75 per cent of the population now use mobile phones. British Airways flies daily to Pristina. Easyjet has established flights from its European hub in Geneva. The tourist potential in this region of rivers, ravines, forests, Alpine hills and delightful lakes, covered in rich verdant green from its fertile fields is enormous. In his Blue Guide to Kosovo, James Pettifer writes: "Prizren, the pearl and Jerusalem of Kosovo, is one of the great historic towns of the Balkans in a magnificent setting at the foot of the Sar mountains. It has outstanding historic buildings from the ancient, medieval and Ottoman periods, and an attractive social and cultural ambience."

One of the best-kept secrets in Europe is the quality of food in Kosovo. At the crossroads of different culinary traditions, the Levantine grills and fresh salads, the Italian pastries, Alpine pork dishes and very decent local wine *vallent le detour* as Michelin might put it.

On a winter visit to southern Kosovo I drove up from Prizren after a delicious lunch to find enticing snow on a 2,000-metre ski valley. I have a passion for skiing and here I could see steep long runs down a perfect skiers' mountain to a welcoming ski village at its foot. It was perfect snow, white, glinting from the setting sun under an Alpine blue sky. But Brezovica, the best ski area south of the Alps, is not attracting snowboarders from Val d'Isère or Verbier further north. Brezovica was once the former Yugoslavia's most popular ski station. Today its rusted snow-covered ski lifts and empty restaurants are emblematic of the economic difficulties created by Belgrade's narrow-minded politics.

The people who live in Brezovica are mostly Serbs. The local Serb mayor wants to see the resort privatised as Swiss, Italian and Austrian investors are ready to make it come to life again.

But politicians in Belgrade insist that ownership of Brezovica is vested in the successors to the old Communist state structures and their offices in Belgrade. Normally a state can decide who owns the land within its frontiers. Kosovo's semi-status makes that difficult.

Investors who would spruce up Brezovica and make it again a prime ski resort have to look over the shoulder at possible legal cases. It is not that they can be sued in Kosovo but if any part of their business involves links with Serbia then their investments there could face a legal challenge. Easier to stay away.

Thus Belgrade punishes the 35,000-strong Serb community of southern Kosovo. Like all mountain communities the people of Brezovica want to get on with their life, make money and develop economic activity like skiing and other winter and summer mountain sports with hotels and restaurants that can provide jobs so that the mountains do not have to be depopulated. Their fellow Serbs in Belgrade prevent this happening.

Bjorn von Sydow was Sweden's Defence Minister and Speaker of the Riksdag, the Swedish parliament. He has visited Kosovo for the Council of Europe and in 2010 reported on his intensive discussions with Serbs in the country:

> More and more Kosovo Serbs in the South are prepared to find a *modus vivendi* with the Kosovo authorities, provided that they are afforded the widest possible autonomy and the highest standards of minority rights, including the right to receive education and deal with the administration in their own language. This trend is also testified by the unexpected increased participation of Kosovo Serbs in the South during the November 2009 local elections.
>
> Serbs living in enclaves in the South told me that they do not have security concerns and can exercise freedom of movement. However, they continue to face serious problems: some of them are common to all communities, such as high

unemployment and untrustworthy judiciary; others are specific to them, such as lack of recognition of documents, and
real or perceived discrimination. In any case, even if there is
no inter-ethnic violence, communities continue to live sepa-
rately and their level of interaction is negligible

Belgrade's efforts to isolate Kosovo economically have hurt
all communities. Kosovan farmers cannot sell the products in
their natural market of southern Serbia. Imagine Welsh lamb
or leeks unable to be traded into England and you have some
idea of how the Belgrade-Moscow policy of denying Kosovo
normal statehood plays out. Convoys of lorries or rail containers full of the organic fruit and vegetables that the fertile
Kosovan plain can produce, especially the warmer climate agricultural produce that northern European supermarkets like to
sell, should be leaving Kosovo daily. Again, the Serb blockade
prevents this.

Despite these obstacles Kosovo has grown more strongly
– albeit from a low base – than most other European nations
since 2001. The EU Commission reported in November 2010
that Kosovo's GDP went up from €1.6 billion to €3.9 billion
between 2001 and 2009. This 140 per cent increase in the size
of the economy was matched by a near doubling of income as
expressed in terms of GDP per capita between 2003 and 2009
which went from €905 to €1790. Of course these figures are
pitifully low by European standards, but we have seen in rural
Ireland, southern Italy, peasant Spain, as well as in the post-
Communist economies that have joined the European Union
remarkably fast growth once barriers to trade and investment
are lifted.

There is no reason not to believe that if the international
community could persuade Belgrade to normalise relations,
Kosovo would develop an economy able to absorb current high
levels of unemployment. This drives many young Kosovan

men either into exile – much as young Irish males had to leave Ireland in the 19th and first half of the 20th century. Or they turn to crime in the manner of southern Italy with its mafias and *cosa nostra* still very much operational as Roberto Saviano described in his brilliant world best-seller *Gomorrah*.

Nonetheless, in a world economy where the new rising economic powers like China, India, Brazil and Turkey are hungry for metals like zinc and lead, companies like Ferronikeli, Kosovo's lead and zinc mining and processing company, are doing well. In the first seven months of 2010, reports the EU, exports of goods increased by a nominal 107 per cent over the same period in 2009.

So-called rare earths have now been discovered in Kosovo. China which controls 95 per cent of the world's rare earths, an essential element in the making of modern components, is opening talks with the Kosovan government with the aim of buying a controlling ownership in the country's rare earth production.

Kosovo is unique amongst nations in that it remains to a large extent a UN and EU protectorate. The EU's 3,000-strong EULEX mission and the 6,300 KFOR troops from the UN provide core security and administrative roles. The 2010 report on Kosovo by the EU is, like previous reports, a long list of what needs to be done.

"Establishing a professional, accountable, accessible, representative public administration and ensuring delivery of public services to all in Kosovo needs to be addressed as a matter of high political urgency", the EU notes. And so say all of us. Residents in Naples, to take just one city, and not a few other cities or remote rural regions in the European Union, might also welcome a "professional, accountable, accessible representative public administration". Indeed, cynics might welcome the day when the EU bureaucracy in Brussels became either accessible or representative.

The EU comments on Kosovo demand from a country which is not allowed to exercise full judicial, policing and security control over all its territory a degree of Nordic-level civil service, media, judicial and economic management norms that are rare to find in many other EU member states, and certainly none in the Balkans. Is Kosovo meant to be inspired by Greece in terms of tax collection? By Croatia in terms of corruption of the prime minister's office? By Italy, in terms of media freedom and independence? In July 2011, the London *Daily Telegraph* compared the Metropolitan Police to the police in Palermo as the full extent of occult payments to British police officers and the collusion of some of them in illegal activities by editors and journalists started to be revealed. Policing and justice in Kosovo need massive improvement as they do in every Balkan state but it is hard after what the British have learnt about their own police, press and politicians to adopt a superior posture.

In fact, Kosovo is struggling to develop the norms of a poor but responsible and democratic rule-of-law state. Take, for example, the problem of managing its borders. Kosovo has 605 kilometres of frontiers and fifteen international border crossings. In April 2010, the Kosovo Border Police took over responsibility from KFOR for patrolling and managing the frontier with Albania. 127 new border guards were recruited.

The Kosovo Border Police are now in charge of all international crossing points into neighbouring countries save the two crossing points into Serbia north of Mitrovica. Here the EU maintains a presence but Serbia maintains its fiction that Kosovo is part of Serbia and refuses to cooperate on a government-to-government basis to ensure internationally recognized flow of traffic from one country to another. It is a recipe and open invitation for smuggling. By contrast, Pristina Airport is modern and its future ownership under the same consortium that runs the highly successful Lyon airport in France will ensure Kosovo's European and international links even if Serbia blocks normal road access. In addition to British Airways, Austrian Air, Lufthansa, Swiss, SAS and Easyjet from Switzerland all fly into Pristina with more than one million passengers a year.

Kosovo has major problems of modernisation to overcome. Laws are passed but not fully implemented. There is criminal pressure on the judicial system. Politicians have incomes, which do not correspond to their formal state incomes. Minorities, including Roma, are badly treated as they are elsewhere in Balkan and Central European states like the Czech Republic, Slovakia, Bulgaria and Romania itself.

The pro-Roma activist, Paul Polanksy, has recorded the appalling suffering of Kosovan Roma kept in a UN camp in northern Kosovo in the region controlled by Belgrade. Nearly 100 of them died from lead poisoning. Roma children are still there, the lead slowly accumulating in their bodies like an unseen poison that will disfigure, maim and eventually kill them. Pristina's writ does not run in this part of Kosovo and anti-Roma racism together with the failure of UNMIK allowed this tragedy to develop.

In any decent world, Pristina and Belgrade would have cooperated to relocate the children away from the source of contamination. But such is Belgrade's dislike of acknowledging the right of Pristina to exercise authority over all of Kosovan territory that the resettlement camps continued to poison Roma families until finally the EU and the US overruled both the Serbs in the Mitrovica region and the anti-Roma sentiments of many Kosovans and brought the Roma community back to the rebuilt villages from where they had been expelled in the fighting of 1999.

But it is not just Roma who want relocation. Kosovans still form the highest percentage of asylum seekers in relation to the size of the country in the EU. In 2009, 14,275 Kosovans applied for asylum in EU member states. This is fewer than the 20,455 Afghanis or 20,095 Russians but more than the 10,470

Georgians or 9,935 Pakistanis. To be sure, many of the Kosovan asylum seekers are economic migrants but as the Robert Bosch Foundation noted in a report, "Kosovo's minorities face harassment, intimidation and sporadic violence". Germany has signed a readmission agreement with Kosovo and is deporting 14,400 Kosovan citizens of whom 9,842 are Roma, 1,755 Ashkali and 173 Egyptian (Ashkali and Egyptian minorities are Roma who speak Albanian while Kosovan Roma are often Serb speakers).

Kosovo's media are ranked alongside those of Serbia, Croatia and Albania as "partly free" in the annual ranking of press freedom produced by the New York based Freedom House. There are able, energetic young journalists in Pristina. As a former president of the British National Union of Journalists I enjoy the raw enthusiasm of young men and women who remind me of my early days as a journalist. But they need more mature structures to work within. Kosovo should seek to buy in newspaper and radio owners from elsewhere in Europe and offer tax and other advantages to build a vibrant media.

The EU has praised the creation and work of the Independent Media Commission but warned that the failure to create a licensing fee or independent financing system for the main Kosovan public service broadcaster, RTK, remains a problem. One of the areas of conflict is between the US view that all media should be privately owned in the style of Rupert Murdoch's biased Fox News and the European tradition that allows space for an independent public service broadcasting tradition, free of proprietorial or political control. Given the political-business nexus and networks in Kosovo, it is important that the country has at least one accepted source of news and discussion, as well as popular programmes people want to watch.

The Serbs in southern and northern Kosovo also need their own media. At the moment this is provided from within Serbia or is provided by the TV Mreza network which links together Serbian-language television stations to provide coverage for

Kosovan Serbs. There is no problem in principle with different language TV and radio stations. Switzerland provides French, German and Italian TV outputs with different editorial and production teams. But if Kosovan Serbs watch television which encourages separatism and a rejection of the common Kosovan Albanian-Serb community with its laws and rules applying throughout the nation, then both the Serbs and Albanians living in Kosovo will suffer.

Again and again there is evidence of Serbian refusal to accept the existence of Kosovo. The Serbian tax authorities issue certificate to Serb firms in Kosovo, which allows them – but not Kosovan Albanian firms – to sell products to Serbia. As the EU notes, "This parallel documentation conflicts with the concept of Kosovo as a single customs area in which only the appropriate Kosovo institutions are empowered to issue such documentation." The EU has criticized Belgrade's refusal to allow goods with custom stamps from Kosovo to enter Serbia.

The story is the same on energy where the EU insists that "As a result of obstruction from Serbia, Kosovo's electricity transmission system operator (KOSTT) continues to find it difficult to participate as an equally partner in regional commercial mechanisms." The parallel society set up by Kosovans to maintain their sense of freedom in the years of Milošević oppression have continued into the 21st century as rule of law is yet to be fully understood or accepted in a society where kinship and clan or ex-KLA loyalties matter greatly.

When I first went to Kosovo as a minister I insisted that independent judges, perhaps from elsewhere in Europe, were needed to impose rough and ready justice. There was and is too much evidence of intimidation of judges or threats to the families of law enforcement and judicial officers. Retired British policemen, notably from Northern Ireland, did come to work in Kosovo paid for by the British government. But they stayed for a short time, did not learn Albanian and while being useful sources of policing experience they were just a small part of a sprawling international community, coming and going, enjoying the allowances and expenses, and sometimes abusing the trust of Kosovan people, especially when it came to sexual favours.

There was never any sense of continuity or of the internationals staying long enough (with some rare and admirable exceptions) to really burrow down and change the modus operandi of Kosovo's law, order and justice activities. I argued that that one of the first things the international community needed to do was focus on security and even create a prison network from which criminals could not be sprung. But as a minister, I was in Kosovo for brief visits and as soon as I was back on the plane my mind drifted to the next problem on my ever-recharging ministerial agenda. This problem of continuity and developing real long-term authoritative leadership presence by the UN, EU and other agencies of the international community remains one of the weakest and most problematic aspects of such work.

In the end, Kosovo cannot be run as a UN or EU protectorate with help from rotating military detachment from NATO armies. As long as Serbia keeps Kosovo hobbled by Belgrade's refusal to accept Kosovo as a neighbour and new partner in the mini-concert of Western Balkan nations, the ambitions of both the people of Kosovo and their friends in the democratic community will be hard to realize. This is why the question of recognizing Kosovo's independence is so important.

9

Smearing Kosovan Politicians

Just before Christmas 2010 a story exploded on the front pages around the world which claimed that the prime minister of Kosovo, Hashim Thaçi, had been a master-mind criminal, involved in the killing of people to extract their kidneys for sale in the late 1990s. Some papers suggested that the organs had been removed from Serbs while they were still alive.

Not since Pol Pot have quite such lurid statements been made about a serving leader of his nation. Thaçi was re-elected in December 2010 with just 34 per cent of the Kosovan voters supporting him, a little less than David Cameron six months previously in Britain, and a lot more than George W. Bush in 2000.

The report that had caused the stir was produced by one of the many sub-committees of the Parliamentary Assembly of the Council of Europe. It was dishonestly presented to the press as if it had the full weight of the Council of Europe, which oversees the European Convention on Human Rights and administers the European Court of Human Rights.

It was written in conjunction with the Council of Europe secretariat by a forceful Swiss-Italian politician-cum-prosecuting lawyer called Dick Marty. He is close to his fellow Italian-Swiss political lawyer, Carla del Ponte, whose 2008 book, *Madame Prosecutor,* made identical allegations to Marty's report. It is not a precise judicial document and contains long rambling denunciations of Western policy as it unfolded in the Kosovo crisis at the end of the 1990s. In it, Marty reflects the politicisation of the Council of Europe, which ever since it admitted Russia as a member in 1995 had been skillfully used by the Kremlin to advance Russian diplomatic interests. Russia has cultivated allies there in different political blocks. In Britain, the Liberal-Democratic MP and Council of Europe member, Mike Hancock, has been accused by the Chair of the British All Party Parliamentary Group on Russia of being flagrantly pro-Kremlin in Council of Europe debates.

The British Conservative MPs on the Council of Europe sit in the same group as Vladimir Putin's hand-picked delegation. The Russians, with the support of British Conservative MPs, sought to place a former KGB staffer as president of the Council of Europe in 2008. In short, the Council of Europe is not some disinterested gathering of Amnesty International or Human Rights Watch parliamentarians, but a deeply conflicted politicised body where states mobilise to promote support for their foreign policy positions.

A top priority for the Kremlin has been to maximize support for anti-US and anti-NATO positions at the Council of Europe. Russia has sought to cultivate allies to protect Serbia and other Slav or Orthodox states from criticism. Efforts by Swedish centrist social democrats to promote reconciliation between Serbs and Kosovans have been rebuffed. Instead of seeking peace and reconciliation there has been a constant effort by the Serb-Russian axis at the Council of Europe to pretend that Kosovo is a criminal gangster breakaway province that one day would return to Serb rule.

Discrediting different Kosovan leaders has been a top political priority for Serbs and Russians. Marty, together with others hostile to the United States on the Council of Europe, has never made any secret of his opposition to Kosovan independence.

He has opposed calls for Kosovo to be given member or even observer status at the Council of Europe. Marty's highly personalized report is the biggest propaganda coup for revanchist Serbs since the fall of Milošević.

Rapporteurs – to give Marty his technical title as author of the report – at the Council of Europe are workaday politicians. There are dozens of such reports each year. Britain's (Lord) Frank Judd was one such rapporteur when he was a delegate. He resigned in disgust when his reports on the brutality of Russia forces under Putin in Chechnya were side-lined by the pro-Moscow alliances in the Council.

Marty is his own man and his sincerity is not up for question. He believes in what he believes. But a reading of his 19,000 word report throws up one problem. There is not one single name or a single witness to the allegations that Thaçi was involved in the harvesting of human organs from murdered victims. Marty says that Kosovans have a clan loyalty that forbids them testifying against leaders. That those disgusting practices happened and happen elsewhere in the world is not in doubt. But Marty fails to link Thaçi directly to organ harvesting though the lurid title of his report – *Illicit trafficking in human organs in Kosovo* – was designed to maximize headlines. The allegations fall within a long-standing tradition of Serb propaganda, which uses the age-old anti-Semitic blood libel (the allegations that people are deliberately killed to use their blood or organs for different purposes) to discredit their opponents. Kemal Kurspahić of the Media in Democracy Institute reported that in the early part of the Balkan conflicts Serbian newspapers were full of horrifying stories about "necklaces of Serbian children's fingers" worn by Croat paramilitaries or Bosnians playing football with the heads of decapitated Serbs. During the siege of Sarajevo a Serb TV station in Bosnia carried a report on "Serb children being fed to the lions in Sarajevo Zoo."

The long-standing Serb allegations against Thaçi, who, as a

young Kosovan leader helped win at Rambouillet the democratic world's support for the liberation of Kosovo, are in this
tradition. Marty does all he can to blacken Thaçi's name, accusing him of being little more than a criminal who used the crisis
of Kosovo chiefly to establish a mafia-style operation. Marty re-
writes history as he opts for the Serb world-view which paints
all Kosovan resistance as essentially and exclusively criminal.
But Thaçi is just one of a number of competing ex-KLA political leaders. There have been thousands of international investi-
gators, police and lawyers operating in Kosovo since 2000. The
Serbs have been unable to produce any victims or families of
people who were killed and then had their kidneys extracted.

In a devastating rebuttal of Marty's claims, Sir Geoffrey
Nice QC, who prosecuted Milošević at The Hague, and who
is a renowned international lawyer, also protested against the
lack of evidence to substantiate Marty's claims. In an article in
the *London Review of Books*, Nice asked if the Marty claims were
"perhaps, part of a media campaign to obstruct the recognition
of Kosovo as an independent state?" I was a British Council
of Europe delegate until 2010. I watched the Serb-Russian axis
at work. No one active in the Council of Europe could have
any doubt about how Belgrade and Moscow sought to create an
atmosphere hostile to Kosovo. Nice has demolished with forensic precision Marty's allegations.

Stories in the Serbian press suggest that many of these allegations came from a witness known as K144. According to media
accounts, K144 has first-hand knowledge of the execution of
Serb prisoners whose kidneys were then removed for sale. The
Serbs have given the impression, without clearly stating it, that
K144 was a "protected witness" of the ICTY. Witnesses sum-
moned for the part of Milošević's trial that dealt with Kosovo
were indeed known by "K" numbers – but they stopped around
K116. If K144 is a genuine pseudonym how did the Serbian

press get to know about it and from whom? Who is K144? The ICTY website has entries for many "K" witnesses, but nothing for K144. According to one newspaper story, K144 claims that there was a trade with vital organs of the kidnapped Kosovo Serbs conducted under direct supervision of Hashim Thaçi and KLA leaders with the consent of Albanian state officials … Doctors would examine all the prisoners and with information from Italy of which organ was needed would decide who would go under a knife … The prisoners were anaesthetised, their organs were extracted, and then they would most often be left to die by being taken off the life support … In several cases the younger prisoners, after having one kidney extracted, were sutured and returned with other prisoners … The biggest mass grave with some 100 Serbs was in … Burrel in central Albania.

Burrel had in fact been investigated by the ICTY during Milošević's trial in 2003–4 after allegations that Serb prisoners had been maltreated there. No conclusive evidence was discovered, although the ICTY was told that there were faint traces of blood in a building known as the Yellow House and that a few, mostly empty, drug containers had also been found.

Secret documents I obtained showed the detailed UN Forensic team's investigation of the so-called Yellow House. Independent scene-of-crime forensic specialists from the US and European countries concluded that there was "no conclusive evidence" that blood traces – whether animal or human – found at the building were "a result of a criminal act." Sir Geoffrey Nice went on:

If K144 had indeed given a statement of the kind Marty suggests before March 2006 – when the Milošević trial ended with the accuser's death – I would have known about it because of its possible ramifications for the prosecution case. Other lawyers would have known too and the information would have had to be handed over to Milošević under tribunal rules.

Another Serb paper, *Večernje Novosti*, has recently printed allegations made by a second witness, someone they call "Lj.K", who claims personal knowledge of what happened. According to her, "a team of surgeons had been making decisions about the removal of organs. Hearts, bone marrow, corneas, kidneys and livers were removed from the kidnapped victims," and the removed organs were transported "in special portable refrigerators by private helicopters". If these accounts have a factual basis one would think that rumours at least would have reached Milošević from the intelligence services, which fed him information that he deployed remorselessly to attack prosecution witnesses. But he never mentioned any trade in organs.

Marty fills his report with information that was based on genuine crimes that had been committed in the region – the dreadful story of the Medicus clinic in Pristina that was used in the sad global buying and selling of human organs. What in most countries is a voluntary gift of a kidney, or some other organ, blood, or part of a healthy body which when transplanted to an ill person can save life or make existence more tolerable has become a financial transaction under globalisation. As a schoolboy in the 1960s hitch-hiking in Europe without much money I sold some blood in Athens. I was healthy and it seemed of little consequence. Today, the poor of the world are offered much bigger sums of money to sell bits of themselves to allow a much richer family or individual to stay alive.

In late 2008 a young Turk, Yilmaz Altun, collapsed at Pristina airport as he was waiting for his flight to Istanbul. He needed urgent medical assistance. A long scar on his back revealed that his kidney had just been removed in a Pristina clinic called the Medicus clinic for transplant to an Israeli citizen. For this operation, he had been promised 15,000 Euros but was never paid. The recipient had paid 80,000 Euros, shared between the doctors who performed the operation.

Investigations carried out in Pristina showed that more than twenty poor Moldovans, Russians and Turks had been brought in to the Medicus clinic in Kosovo in 2008. They were lured by the same false promises of big money compensation. Kosovo's EULEX prosecutors have now indicted two doctors linked to the Medicus clinic – the Turkish surgeon Yusuf Sönmez Ercina and Israel's Moshe Harel. They were charged for "trafficking in persons, organized crime and unlawful exercise of medical activity". So far nine people, including seven Kosovars, have been charged, but no trial date has been set.

For more than a decade Dr Sönmez – dubbed as "*Dr Franken-stein*" in the Turkish media – was involved in numerous cases of organ trafficking. He was arrested January 2011 in his luxurious villa in Istanbul, but later released by the court. In 1996 the Turkish investigative journalist Ugur Dündar described him as the brain of an organized organ trafficking network. In 2007, Yusuf Sönmez was again condemned in Turkey for "illegal transplants", performed in his Istanbul clinic. In the clinic, police found his Israeli partner, Zaki Shapira, and four patients awaiting transplantation. Dr Sönmez flitted between Israel (where elderly sick people do buy organs for transplant even if this is illegal in Israel), Turkey, Azerbaijan and Kosovo as he carried out his organ harvesting trade. In Pristina he earned 6,000 Euros a week.

Although he was the surgeon with links to the families desperate to obtain organs at any price, it was Kosovan businessmen who invested in the clinic, including former KLA members and members of Thaçi's PDK party. One of them, a member of the Kosovo assembly called Shaip Muja, also came up in the media. In his report Marty says Muja played a "major role" for "more than ten years" in international networks that specialise in human trafficking and illegal surgery. Yet Shaip Muja was only heard as a witness, not as an accused person, in the Medicus case. In an interview with *Le Monde* in March 2011, he affirmed he had "no link" with Medicus and had "never encouraged illegal activity."

What Marty was doing in the time-honoured fashion of the smear campaign was to take a disgusting and shocking event in Kosovo – the organ harvesting trade and a criminal operation at the Medicus clinic, which once it was discovered, was closed down – and then link it back to Serb propaganda by alleging that their opponents were the propagators of this crime.

In his Council of Europe report Marty says he has read the many denunciations of Thaçi with "consternation and a sense of moral outrage". He claims that MI6 backs his claims, but again produces no evidence that he has read MI6 reports naming Thaçi and his group. Moral outrage and consternation are important reactions, but should a factual report endorsed by the Council of Europe not have some direct witness statements, some dry facts, some proof, and, find at least one person who can substantiate the link between Thaçi and organ harvesting? Sir Geoffrey Nice is also not persuaded.

Marty, like del Ponte, is a Swiss lawyer – a former prosecutor in the canton of Ticino. His report is not, as he admits, a criminal investigation. It attempts a sweeping survey of Albanian clan life and its relationship with organized crime and argues that the 1998–99 conflict was a gangsters' turf war rather than an insurrection against the Serbs. Organized crime in Kosovo, he asserts, is run by the current political elite, Thaçi included. Marty also makes use of his immunity as a representative of the Council of Europe from pursuit for defamation and sets out details of the two organ harvesting schemes – one by surgery on captives, the other by the swindling of donors. He fails to demonstrate any connection between the two, however, beyond the fact that each involved Kosovan politicians. He suggests that the West was so keen to back the Kosovo Albanians that they could get away with anything – even trading in body parts – under the noses of Western observers.

Marty's report states: "It was in ... Fushë-Krujë [a town in Albania] that the process of 'filtering' purportedly reached its end-point, and the small, select group of KLA captives who were brought this far met their death. There are strong indications, from source testimonies we have obtained, that ... some of these captives became aware of the ultimate fate that awaited them [and] are said to have pleaded with their captors to be spared the fate of being 'chopped into pieces' ... When they were physically examined by men referred to as 'doctors', the captives must have been put on notice that they were being treated as some form of medical commodities ... Captives were killed, usually by a gunshot to the head, before being operated on to remove one or more of their organs ... This was principally a trade in 'cadaver kidneys', i.e. the kidneys were extracted posthumously; it was not a set of advanced surgical procedures requiring controlled clinical conditions and, for example, the extensive use of anaesthetic ... As and when the transplant surgeons were confirmed to be in position and ready to operate, the captives were brought out of the 'safe house' individually, summarily executed by a KLA gunman, and their corpses transported swiftly to the operating clinic."

Marty doesn't explain why this expensive process – doctors and intermediaries would have had to be paid enough to ensure they kept quiet, helicopters would have had to be hired – would have seemed a better idea than, say, the lucrative trade in smuggled tobacco in which Montenegro and Serbia as well as Kosovo have long been involved, or the drug trade.

Given all this, has Thaçi succeeded in avoiding justice? Other KLA leaders have had to stand trial and a few of them are to be re-tried, including Ramush Haradinaj, who is accused of witness tampering at his first trial. One suggested explanation for why Thaçi was not charged is that Madeleine Albright ordered the tribunal not to indict him; del Ponte says there was insufficient evidence against him. So why did his name suddenly become attached to the allegations about the organ trade, probably the least plausible of the many he has faced? Why does del Ponte claim that he could not have been tried at the ICTY? Executing and butchering prisoners of war during or immediately after an armed conflict would certainly qualify as a war crime. The cut-off date for new indictments at the tribunal was January 2004, but something as serious as these alleged crimes might have been given special dispensation by the UN. The evidence should, in any event, have been dealt with by the tribunal and not published in a memoir. Appearing two years after del Ponte's book, the Marty report doesn't go beyond the rumours she made public and which Serb websites and newspapers have been repeating and embellishing ever since. Marty keeps his sources hidden for fear – we are told – that they might be harmed by the Kosovans involved or even by Albanians more generally.*

Thaçi himself immediately called for a full and independent investigation into the allegations. The Russians and Serbs applied for a UN Commission of Inquiry. This was rejected as it was clearly a political stunt aimed at Kosovo's political leader. But in June 2011, Moscow again tried to get the UN to carry out its own investigation as part of the Kremlin's anti-Kosovo crusade.

Mr Marty's attack on Thaçi shows the continuing refusal to accept that the Balkan wars, including the repression and violence against the people of Kosovo, now belong in the 20th-century history books. It is time for Kosovo and Serbia to move on. But for many in Belgrade, together with their allies in the Council of Europe, repeating the allegations of the past is more important than building a peaceful Balkans in the future. Dick Marty is now retiring from the Council of Europe and the upper house of the Swiss Parliament. It is sad that his last act was to smear someone without producing any proof. The Council of Europe will move on to other subjects and try and forget about the disgraceful smear without any evidence that was given such prominence because it was presented to the world not as Mr Marty's personal opinion but as a report published in the name of the Council of Europe.

In July 2011 the EULEX mission in Kosovo set up its own inquiry with senior lawyers from different countries sitting on it. It will take a year or more to produce a report, which – unless Marty does produce real evidence – will have to conclude that the Council of Europe colluded in a political character assassination of which its leaders and secretariat should be ashamed. The Serbs and Russians have already achieved their propaganda victory as respectable media bodies like the *Sunday Times* and Germany second television network, ZDF, repeat the Marty allegations without examining or challenging them. A lie had got all the way around the world before the truth could catch up.

10

Recognition – the Way Forward

The propaganda against Kosovo and its leaders pours out of Belgrade with the active backing of Moscow for one reason. Both Serbs and Russian have erected into a high point of their international policy the refusal to recognize Kosovo. Serbia wants to have influence, control even, over those areas of the Balkans – Kosovo, Bosnia-Herzegovina and Montenegro – where communities of Serbs live. This flies against the core European principle established after 1945 that European borders would not be reformatted save with the express will of all peoples and governments involved as happened in the peaceful divorce between the Czech Republic and Slovakia. Serbia's ultra-nationalist line is blocking progress in the Balkans. If the European Union is true to its values the Serb obduracy will prevent Serbia becoming an EU member state in contrast to Croatia which accepted a peaceful outcome to a dispute with Slovenia about the latter's access to the Adriatic.

The continuing refusal of Belgrade to negotiate openly and honestly with Kosovo on a friendly and final peace settlement stopped the normalisation of Kosovo as a small Balkan state in the first decade of the 21st century. In contrast to Serbia, where politics were scarred by violence including the assassination of a Prime Minister, the politicians in Kosovo held elections and government control moved between parties.

In contrast to Albania where elections were openly stolen by the ruling party, the Constitutional Court in Pristina has ordered re-runs of elections and even forced a nominated president to stand down. Also in contrast to Serbia, where indicted war criminals eluded capture for years with Ratko Mladić not being arrested and sent to The Hague until May 2011, Kosovan leaders wanted by ICTY voluntarily agreed to go there. These even included the elected Prime Minister Ramush Haradinaj who stood down as Prime Minister in 2005 to go to The Hague.

Sir Geoffrey Nice QC questioned the indictment of the Kosovan leader. The view amongst the international experts in The Hague was that the ambitious and highly politicised Swiss chief prosecutor, Carla Del Ponte, felt obliged to issue the warrant against Haradinaj. She was under pressure from the constant complaints by Serbs, who have an important network linked to secret bank accounts in Swiss banks, that The Hague tribunal was only keen on prosecuting Serbs and not Kosovans.

In fact Haradinaj's stay in The Hague was short-lived as there was simply no good evidence that could be found to prosecute him. He had asked me privately whether he should go there and I urged him to do so. In contrast, the nationalist Serb political milieu and their media continually portrayed the search for justice following the war crimes of the 1990s as the world ganging up against the valiant people of Serbia and their heroes like Radovan Karadžić and Ratko Mladić.

By the end of 2005 it was clear that Kosovo's future status had to be decided once and for all and that it could not limp along under the unhappy guidance of the UN administration for ever. Finland's former president and Nobel Peace Prize Laureate, Martti Ahtisaari, was charged by the UN to try and find a solution. In the course of 2006 Ahtisaari engaged in a series of meetings and even persuaded the new Serb President, Boris Tadić and the Prime Minister Vojislav Koštunica to come and meet their Kosovan opposite numbers in Vienna.

Koštunica had been an opponent of Milošević. But he was a nationalist constitutional lawyer who insisted that the Serb constitutional settlement obliged every elected Serb politician to keep Kosovo within the orbit of Belgrade's rule. He was friendly enough to talk to and reminded me of what Winston Churchill called "stiff-necked Ulstermen" – men opposed to violence, without any direct malevolence or vindictiveness in their hearts, but utterly incapable of understanding that their version of how all the people of Northern Ireland should live placed the Catholic-Nationalist minority in a permanently inferior category. So too Koštunica was a man of honour and dignity and personal integrity and yet so narrow-minded in his insistence on the Serbian right to rule that he was in his time of office a major obstacle to peace.

He was succeeded by Boris Tadić, one of the most likeable and liked politicians in Europe. I met him as defence minister, and then president, a post he was elected to in 2004 in his mid-40s. He was tall, friendly, easy to talk to but had the dignity and bearing of a statesman. Now aged 53, he is a great warm bear of a man linked to all the social democratic parties in Europe and very popular at their congresses and meetings.

Tadić's commitment to a reformed modern and European Serbia was never in doubt. He went to Bosnia and Croatia to apologise for Serb crimes committed in those countries. When pressed at social democratic gatherings or privately by friends he avoids the harsh language he uses to placate nationalist voters inside Serbia. But allowing Kosovo to be Kosovo appears to be a step too far. So far he has been unable to find language that would lead the Serbs to a better place on the Balkan political landscape.

Despite dealing with Martti Ahtisaari, one of the cleverest bridge-builders between seemingly incompatible positions, Tadić refused to cross the bridge to peace with Kosovo that the former Finnish president designed during the talks of a final settlement in the course of 2006. Ahtisaari decided in the end to make his own recommendations and in February 2007 put forward his proposals for a settlement on the question of status.

There were classic safeguards for the non-Albanian communities in Kosovo and for the heritage sites of the Serbian Orthodox Church. Ahtisaari skillfully avoided the word 'independence' but made clear that Kosovo would become a member of international organizations like the UN or the Council of Europe and have its own flag and the other symbols of a nation state including its own security force or army.

It was not a propitious moment. George W. Bush was bogged down in Iraq and Afghanistan. US diplomatic energy was at its lowest ebb. France and Britain were losing two strong chiefs – Jacques Chirac and Tony Blair – who had been fully engaged in European, including Balkan, politics, in the way their successors were not. The EU was wrangling over the terms of what became the Lisbon Treaty.

Moscow now stepped into the dispute and said a very firm *Niet* to any settlement for Kosovo that was not approved by Belgrade. This show of support for Belgrade was not simply a question of solidarity. Vladmir Putin's increasingly nationalistic and aggressive foreign policy derived its confidence from rising revenue from the mono-economy of energy and was engaged in a sequence of disputes with the West. During the Orange Revolution in Ukraine the candidate that Putin had gone in person to support was defeated. The victorious pro-Western president was allegedly poisoned by Russian agents. Even if the Ukrainian reform movement disintegrated thanks to personal squabbles and internal bickering, Ukraine's rejection of Russian leadership had been a humiliating moment for the Kremlin.

There had also been a trade war with Poland when Russia unilaterally banned the export of Polish pork products. It was a childish move and Poland had the support of its EU partners who initiated their own countermeasures forcing the Kremlin to back down. In Estonia, Russia launched a cyber war, shutting down the IT-dependent state administration in Estonia. The pretext was a dispute over the relocation of a Russian war memorial. It was a cynical pretext as Moscow sought reasons to have a row with the small Baltic States. Estonia with a population smaller than that of Kosovo was an easy target.

Russia also found unacceptable the arrival in power after the so-called Rose Revolution of Mikheil Saakashvili in Georgia. He set about an energetic reform of the corrupt Georgian state administration including the dismissal of every single policeman so that Georgia became the only country in the region where the police did not demand bribes. He also liberalised the economy and said that Georgia should become a member of both the European Union and NATO following the path of the Baltic and East European states which had entered NATO and the EU.

Putin stepped up the pressure on Georgia and declared that it was a strategic goal of Russia to stop the small Black Sea nation integrating fully with the West. He compared South Ossetia, the northern region of Georgia, with Kosovo. South Ossetia has about seventy thousand inhabitants and has become a fiefdom of Russian mafia gangs working with former KGB officers.

Georgia's handling of its different regions since conflicts in the early 1990s certainly left a lot to be desired. But there was no comparison with Kosovo, which is an authentic nation dominated by a majority population with other minorities. Putin used the Serb Kosovo difference as a way of Russia showing its power at the United Nations.

All during 2007 the United States and the European Union, working closely with UN officials, bent over backwards to find fine language that would both allow Kosovo its right to be a state while maintaining a strong international supervisory presence there. The European Union agreed to take over from UNMIK responsibility for rule of law and set up its EULEX mission.

Diplomatists at the United Nations drafted and then rewrote four times a UN resolution that could replace UN Resolution 1244 which had left the status of Kosovo unclear and under the control of Serbia.

However, Kosovo's fate was now being decided in the Kremlin. Belgrade's political leaders were able to hide behind the Russian decision to assert Russia's own status as a major world power by denying the people of Kosovo their right to nationhood. For the Russian zero-sum view of international relations in which concessions are only made in exchange for other concessions being granted, the fate of Kosovo was of little importance. Russia was at loggerheads with the Bush administration's policy in Iraq and its proposals to set up a missile defence shield as part of the new NATO concern about attacks from Iranian missiles, which could soon, it was feared, be equipped with nuclear warheads.

By the end of 2007 it was clear that Russia was not prepared to help bring peace to the Balkans but would prefer to maintain the non-status of Kosovo in order to show its continuing authority at the United Nations. Either the democratic world had to buckle to the refusal of Belgrade to negotiate recognition of Kosovo as the other nations of the former Yugoslavia had achieved, and accept the obstructionism of the Kremlin. Alternatively the EU, America and their allies could decide enough was enough and consider that Kosovo was independent. Ahtisaari was rewarded with the Nobel Peace Prize in part for his work in trying to persuade Belgrade that the time was right to move forward on Kosovo. Nobel Peace Prizes – rightly – are awarded not for achieving peace but for "the best work for fraternity between nations" as the Nobel Peace Prize definition puts it. Ahtisaari had toiled tirelessly to promote fraternity between the Serb and Kosovan nations. But Belgrade's politicians were not yet ready to become friends with the country their predecessors had colonized.

His frustration was shared by the Swiss Foreign Minister,

Micheline Calmy-Rey, who had long campaigned for Kosovo to become independent. She made the point at the UN, as well as in editorials and interviews in European papers like *Le Monde* and *Tages Anzeiger*. Both Finland and Switzerland were outside NATO, and had cultivated the reputation as moderate, neutral states that could broker agreements in difficult geopolitical cases. Both Ahtisaari and Calmy-Rey were rebuffed by Belgrade. In July 2005, Serb President Tadić told Calmy-Rey that "he was not open to discussion about independence for Kosovo". But the Swiss socialist veteran politician stood her ground. As she said in 2010, ten per cent of the Kosovan population had sought refuge and was now living in Switzerland. Berne understood the need for self-determination and independence so that, as Calmy-Rey put it, "The region could be stabilised."

The Kosovans waited politely until after Serbia's presidential election in January 2008 and on 17 February 2008 voted overwhelmingly for independence, nearly a decade after the end of hostilities in the territory. Their statement declared:

> We, the democratically elected leaders of our people, hereby declare Kosovo to be an independent and sovereign state. This declaration reflects the will of our people and it is in full accordance with the recommendations of UN Special Envoy Martti Ahtisaari and his Comprehensive Proposal for the Kosovo Status Settlement. We declare Kosovo to be a democratic, secular and multi-ethnic republic, guided by the principles of non-discrimination and equal protection under the law.

The eleven Serb members of the Assembly boycotted the vote but the nine members representative of other ethnic minorities voted in favour.

The Serb reaction was predictable. Violent protests were

organized in Mitrovica. Bishop Artemije, the head of the Serbian Orthodox church in Kosovo, used somewhat unclerical language when he preached that "Serbia should buy state-of-the-art weapons from Russia and other countries and call on Russia to send volunteers and establish a military presence in Serbia." Serbia's nationalist prime minister, Vojislaw Koštunica, attacked Washington for being "ready to violate the international order for its own military interests" and added "As long as the Serb people exist, Kosovo will be Serbia." In fact, the worry was the opposite – that the US would pull out of Kosovo completely leaving the impoverished European members of NATO to invest more soldiers in the region.

In a theatrical gesture Belgrade issued arrest warrants for high treason against Kosovo leaders and announced all ambassadors would be withdrawn from countries that recognized Kosovo. Today 80 of the world's states, including all the leading democracies, have diplomatic relations with Kosovo. Serbia has not closed its embassies in London, Paris or Washington. Belgrade also unleashed a wave of thuggish violence with attacks on the US embassy in Belgrade, as well as on that great symbol of America, McDonalds.

American diplomats were withdrawn for their own safety and the UN reminded Serbia of its duty to protect embassies. Once again the raw violent nationalism of the Serbs was on display. This over-reaction only won more support for Kosovo. Sensibly this bluster and violence was replaced by an appeal to international law – as there was little doubt that the act of independence did not resolve the absence of a UN resolution accepting Kosovo as a member state.

International lawyers, like any other lawyers, can produce convincing arguments for both sides, or more, of any question. The issue of Kosovan independence was no different. Belgrade referred the independence of Kosovo to the International Court of Justice in The Hague. In July 2010, the ICJ ruled that the declaration of independence did not violate international law. This was a blow to Belgrade and was greeted in Pristina by the Kosovan prime minister, Hashim Thaçi, saying there would be no "winners or losers" as a result of the ICJ ruling.

Thaçi was right to be cautious. Despite the ICJ ruling Moscow and Belgrade continue to deny Kosovo the status of a nation-state. It is difficult to see why. A wide variety of nations have recognized Kosovo. These include not just the participants in the 1999 war but Arab states like Jordan, Bahrain and Saudi Arabia. Former Yugoslav nations like Slovenia, Croatia and Macedonia as well as Balkan neighbours like Bulgaria recognize Kosovo. States in Latin America include Honduras, Colombia and Costa Rica who all accept Kosovo's independence. Majority Muslim countries like Turkey, Malaysia and Indonesia as well as the big Asia Pacific economies – Japan, South Korea and Australia – all now see Kosovo as a partner in the community of nations.

But there are major holes. Take Europe. The decision by Kosovo to declare independence in February 2008 was one thing. Sequencing the recognition of Kosovo by other states was another. Here, as so often in the George W. Bush years, American diplomacy was a contradiction in terms. Washington put pressure on its allies to move swiftly to recognize Kosovo. Unfortunately this coincided with the climax of the closely-fought Spanish election. Madrid politicians in all parties were placed in an impossible position.

The Spanish conservative opposition party, *Partido Popular* (PP), had made a theme of its opposition in its argument that the ruling socialist (PSOE) government had given too many concessions to regional and national groupings within Spain. More than 800 Spaniards had been murdered by the extreme nationalist terror organization, ETA. There was no violence in Catalonia but the Catalans insisted on a great deal of autonomy and talked openly of independence. The PP was ultra-centralist and

PSOE politicians believed that if they agreed to recognize Kosovo they would be accused of supporting secessionist and independentist politics with a clear read-across to Spain.

The dominant figure in the PP is its former leader and prime minister, José Maria Aznar. He was personal friend and ideological soul-mate of George W. Bush. Between 2004 and 2008, Aznar met President George W. Bush more often than Spain's socialist prime minister. Washington failed to use this proximity to urge Aznar to encourage a bi-partisan approach on the issue of Kosovo recognition.

Moreover, the Spanish foreign minister at the time, Miguel Angel Moratinos, had been courted by the Serbs. His first diplomatic posting had been Belgrade. The city made him an honorary freeman. Serb politicians and diplomats applauded the anti-American tone of some Spanish diplomacy after Spain abruptly withdrew its troops from Iraq when the Socialists won power in March 2004. Moratinos announced in Brussels that Spain would not recognize Kosovo and once the formal declaration was made it would prove to be difficult to change the policy.

Many foreign policy experts in Madrid as well as politicians of the right and the left privately agree that Spain's non-recognition policy is counter-productive. Spain proclaims itself the most European and EU-oriented of the major European nation-states. Yet while all the major EU counties have recognized Kosovo Spain has destroyed the hopes of a coherent EU foreign policy position on the Western Balkans.

Diplomats at the United Nations mutter that Spain goes further. Madrid, goes the accusation, has actively campaigned, especially in Latin America where the Spanish diplomatic network is the strongest of any European country, to discourage Latin American capitals from recognizing Kosovo.

The paradox is that of all the Western European nations, Spain, and in particular the Spanish left, should have the most understanding of and sympathy for Kosovo. The activities and ideology of Milošević and his oppression of the rights of Kosovan so closely resembles that of the Franco era as to be uncanny. The brutality of Franco's soldiers, the torture, killings and expulsions of republican Spaniards after the civil war is analogous to the sufferings of the Kosovans under Milošević.

It might be thought that if any nation should have an instinctive solidarity with Kosovo it would be Spain. Perhaps because the cause of Kosovo was backed by the United States, which after 1945 did nothing to support Spanish democrats and socialists against Franco, there is a feeling amongst Spanish policy-makers that to support Kosovo is to endorse a made-in-Washington policy. In fact, as this book has tried to argue, the US was indifferent to the plight of Kosovo until the last possible moment. Even then, it required European leadership from Tony Blair to persuade President Clinton to act.

Whatever the reason, Spain has dealt a serious blow to the idea of a common European foreign policy by its decision to endorse Serb irredentism. Madrid is cut off from major EU capitals like Paris, Berlin, Paris, Rome and Warsaw. With a change of government possibly the PP and PSOE can agree to make Kosovo a bi-partisan issue but given the highly conflicted nature of Spanish politics this is unlikely.

Two Orthodox EU member states, Greece and Cyprus, also refuse recognition out of solidarity with the Orthodox Church in Serbia, though Orthodox Macedonia has recognized Kosovo. The Vatican also refuses to offer diplomatic recognition to Kosovo. The most famous Albanian, born in Skopje (Shkup), is Mother Theresa who many Catholics revere as a saint – she has already been beatified. Kosovo's first president, Ibrham Rugova, supported the building of the Mother Teresa Cathedral in the centre of Pristina and is believed by many to have converted to Catholicism from Islam shortly before his death. It seems thus a little churlish for the Vatican to snub Kosovo. But the Roman

Church thinks and acts in centuries not in decades so Vatican recognition may have to wait.

Bratislava and Bucharest have also said no to recognition. This has only lost both capitals the respect of foreign-policy makers elsewhere in Europe. The formal reason is that Romania and Slovakia fear the nationalist claims from Budapest over the Hungarian-speaking areas of Romania and Slovakia. Unfortunately, the EU appears unable to stop the vulgar nationalist language of the Hungarian right as they assert claims to Slovakian and Romanian territory where Hungarian ethnic groups live.

But the rest of EU member states all recognize Kosovo. Eighty countries now recognize Kosovo, including all the major world democracies. Britain's Foreign Secretary, William Hague, told the House of Commons in June 2011 that Serbia and Kosovo should start a dialogue to "move both states with the view of both entering the EU." Belgrade will not do so as long it has Spain's support on the non-recognition of Kosovo. Russia also will not help resolve the question of Kosovo's entry into the United Nations unless it lets fall the Serb pawn as part of a bigger move on the global chessboard where big powers play out their rivalries at the expense of small nations.

After the arrest of Ratko Mladić, the 'Butcher of Srebenica', the final closure of the terrible Milošević years seemed to be at hand. Yet in his hour of triumph as he presented the world with the news that Mladić had been arrested, Serbia's president Tadić managed to create problems. Mladić's arrest happened on the eve of a major gathering of East European and Balkan leaders in Warsaw to meet in conference with President Obama. Tadić could have arrived in Warsaw crowned in glory as the leader who had finally helped bring an end to the Mladić saga. But he refused to go to Warsaw because Poland, as host state, had invited the presidents of all the Balkan nations including Kosovo's new young president, Atifete Jahjaga, the first woman head of state in the Balkans.

This was a major error. Obama's key foreign policy advisers, as well as US Vice-President Joe Biden, Secretary of State, Hilary Clinton, and UN Ambassador Susan Rice are children of the 1990s who watched in frustration as neither the UN nor the EU were able to stop the genocidal slaughter of Srebrenica nor the mass killings of Kosovan Muslims by Serb paramilitaries.

Getting Obama to Warsaw was a remarkable coup for Radek Sikorski, Poland's single-minded, outspoken but strategic Foreign Minister. Oxford-educated Sikorksi has moved on from a 1980s neo-conservatism to his position today as Europe's most innovative and creative foreign minister. He has helped reduce the age-old Poland enmity of its two neighbours, Russia and Germany, to manageable, even friendly, relationships.

He has more contacts in Washington than any other European politician and he parleyed these into Obama's major visit. To place Poland as the pivot of Euro-Atlantic politics in the new Europe, Sikorski invited all European nations to come and talk with Obama. On Kosovo, Sikorski was very clear. "Kosovo is recognized by some 76 countries, including the majority of the European Union. Poland recognizes Kosovo so there was no reason not to invite Kosovo's representative," Sikorski told the *Financial Times*. He had a blunt message for Serbia's President Boris Tadić. "Serbia has to show that is has overcome the demons from its past if it wants to join the European Union."

In fact, the EU's foreign affairs chief, Kathy Ashton, has been quietly effective in trying to bring Belgrade and Pristina together. Her chief aide, the able British diplomatist, Robert Cooper, has been involved in quasi-shuttle diplomacy between Brussels, Belgrade and Pristina. Writing in the *Guardian* after Mladić's arrest, Baroness Ashton, urged the Serb president, Boris Tadić, to show leadership. She wrote:

I look to Tadić to show the same boldness and generosity in dealing with the even more complicated issue of Kosovo. I know he has willing partners in Pristina.

We should not be starry eyed about the region. Differences remain. Politics could fail. Violence could return. But nor should we retreat into hand-wringing pessimism. Virtually everyone I have spoken to on my visits wants the EU to play a more active role. I tell them we are happy to do that. But I also tell them there is something we cannot do. Leadership – a vision of the future and a readiness to take risks for it – is the mystery ingredient that foreigners cannot supply.

Aristotle said the state is a moral entity. Its transformation needs moral leadership. There is real hope that, with EU membership the prize, this kind of leadership is beginning to spread across the Balkans. Our challenge, and it is a tough one, is to help it last.

Balkan observers also query whether Belgrade is stringing Moscow along. Russia wants to exercise strategic oversight in the Balkans and refuses to deal with the EU as an entity preferring bilateral relationships with EU member states. Yet Serbia's ambition and interest has to lie in becoming a full EU member state. Thus, runs the argument, Belgrade is using Russia until it obtains a road map for EU membership negotiations without first recognising Kosovo. The question of who is duping whom fascinates those who watch the moves on the political chessboard in the Balkans. In the end the EU will make a strategic mistake if the European Council and Commission entertain EU membership for Serbia without first obtaining Belgrade's recognition of Kosovo and an end to Serb meddling in Bosnia and Montenegro.

Smart Serbs know the pretence that Kosovo is just a breakaway province that will come to accept rule or oversight from Belgrade is a fiction. But they resile from the "boldness and generosity" that the EU's foreign policy supremo urges upon them. The choice is simple. Either Belgrade throws in its lot with Russia and turns against Europe and the Euro-Atlantic community. Or somehow Serb politicians rise above old hates, rather like nationalist and unionist Irish politicians did, or, on a grander scale, French and German leaders achieved after 1945.

Under the auspices of the European Union's External Action Service, talks are taking place between Pristina and Belgrade. The latest round in July 2011 produced modest results. Serbia agreed to provide Kosovo with copies of land registers, which had been illegally removed from Pristina to Belgrade in 1999. Aspects of decent living such as obtaining a divorce or, in the criminal field, cracking down on identity theft have been made difficult by Serbia's retention of these records. There was no political gain to Belgrade by holding on to the birth and marriage certificates of Kosovan citizens – both Serb and Albanian. It was low-grade spite. Cars from Kosovo can now travel through Serbia but only if they buy special licence plates at Serbian border posts as Belgrade finds the banal and boring Kosovan car number plates an intolerable presence on Serbian soil. In a decision worthy of Monty Python, Serb officials will recognize Kosovan identity cards but not passports. The distinction is meaningless as ID cards are valid travel documents in many EU countries.

Nonetheless the tireless bridge-building work by Baroness Ashton's chief diplomatic aide, Robert Cooper, was an important advance by the EU's new foreign policy team. Individual governments in Washington, London, Paris or Moscow had not been able to advance the Serb-Kosovan relationship much beyond where it was after the expulsion of Milošević's men in 1999. Twelve years later, the EU had began easing some tensions. But the substantive problem of the lack of full nation-state status for Kosovo continues to plague the Western Balkans. Serbia's obduracy makes a swift adherence to the EU so much more difficult.

Thus the democratic world community, starting with Spain, which received so much European solidarity to overcome the Franco years, needs to accelerate the recognition of Kosovo. The western Balkans has a bad reputation as a region that produces only problems, never solutions. Letting Kosovo be Kosovo would be a good solution to a centuries-old problem.

Conclusion

A 21st-Century Future for Kosovo

The tragedy of all politics is that until there is a crisis no one knows there is a problem. On the whole, at the end of their first decade of existence free of Belgrade's control, Kosovans are not a problem. They do not riot or challenge international troops and officials. Their reward for this peace and normality is to be ignored by the international community. Greece was corruptly governed by governments that lied to themselves, to the Greeks and to the European Union about the state of the nation's budget and tax system until an honest politician, George Papandreou, arrived and the global financial markets dug deeper into the horrors of Greek public financing. The Greek problem became a crisis without any interval.

So too, in the 1990s, no one noticed that a disaster was developing in Kosovo until the flood of asylum seekers reached biblical proportion and the rampaging of the Serb army and paramilitaries could not be hidden any longer. Today, Kosovo is without open conflict. In contrast to Serbia, where a popular reformist president was shot dead in 2004, Kosovan politics has not given rise to violence. In 2004 there were riots in Kosovo but they were contained. No one has tried to use violence against the Serbs bankrolled by Belgrade to maintain control of Mitrovica and its hinterland. There have been riots and deaths in Albania because of the election-stealing by the ruling elite there. In Kosovo, elections are re-run and elected officials dismissed by an independent court. Serb rioting in Belgrade in 2008 or in Mitrovica in 2011 was more murderous and caused more damage than anything seen in Kosovo in recent years.

Kosovans are accused of many failings. But criminality and corruption can be found in many corners of European politics. Without the complicity of banks that hide laundered cash from crime or the demand by upright northern European men for sex with trafficked girls the criminals would not flourish so easily. Every request for extradition to The Hague has been met swiftly by Kosovo. Contrast that with the years of protection the Serb state gave to Serb war criminals or the bluster by Croatian officials about their war criminals.

Europe prided itself a little over a decade ago on bringing the Milošević terror to an end. In June 2011 Carl Bildt, Sweden's Foreign Minister, tweeted that Slovenia and Croatia were celebrating 20 years of independence. Bildt is one of the best EU foreign policy thinkers – and, more importantly, doers. But the question has to be asked again and again, why has the EU been unable to allow effective independence for Kosovo?

Europe has allowed Kosovo to slip down the agenda. President Obama has met the president of Kosovo in Warsaw and the US does its best. But in the greater game of world politics, Washington needs Moscow's support to wind down the war in Afghanistan and help contain Iran's drive to become a nuclear-armed state under the control of Jew-hating religious fundamentalists.

There have been many proposals to try and get round Serbia's obduracy. Alexandros Mallias, one of Greece's most distinguished ambassadors, surveyed the Kosovo problem in 2010 for the Athens-based foreign policy think-tank, Eliamp (The Hellenic Foundation for Europe and Foreign Policy). Eliamp experts had warned in the 1990s that Kosovo needed to be defused before it exploded. But they were not listened to despite the very great expert knowledge Greeks have of their Northern Balkan neighbours.

Athens is not taken seriously as a constructive force in EU foreign policy circles because of its Lilliputian dispute with Macedonia over the right of Macedonia to call itself Macedonia. This is curious as Greece's socialist prime minister, George Papandreou, was one of the most courageous of the region's politicians when, as Foreign Minister, he reversed the longstanding hostility Greece had towards Turkey and, instead, reached out to Ankara on a partnership basis. Tadić could usefully imitate Papandreou's détente policy towards Turkey and reach out to Kosovo. And Greece could encourage Tadić by taking the important step of recognising Kosovo's right to exist.

Ambassador Mallias sets out the problem clearly: "Kosovo and Serbia, Kosovar Albanians and Serbs will live together. Whatever the outcome of the talks, Serbia will be Kosovo's neighbour and Kosovo will be Serbia's neighbour. From the few, limited options they have, the best is to create the conditions for the next generation." Mallias suggests what he calls "The Next Generation Initiative" which would be useful if European cultural and civil-society organizations like the British Council, the Open Society Foundation, and the German and Nordic political foundations could come together to create a generous programme to allow young Serbs and Kosovans to meet. Beginning outside their respective countries they could find what unites them rather than live with the language of generations still passionate about the differences of the past. Serbs and Kosovans must live with their past but should not live in the past.

To achieve this, the European Commission must reach out to 2 million Kosovans with the offer of visa-free or easy-visa travel to Europe. Any Kosovan who wants to come and live in Europe under the claim of being an asylum seeker can do so easily enough. The EU allows bad policy to drive out good policy. Illegal movement of Kosovans is easy. Legal movement of Kosovans faces difficulties. This should be reversed. Kosovan Albanian is now Switzerland's fourth language as so many have moved there legally or illegally. Pristina cooperates fully with European capitals in taking back fake Kosovan asylum seekers.

On the surface, Brussels appears positive about easing Kosovans' access to travel. In November 2010, the European Commission declared it was "committed to launch a visa liberalisation dialogue (with Kosovo) shortly." But so far not much has happened. Europe is more relaxed about giving visa-free access to Taiwan which no EU member state recognizes as an independent state than helping Kosovo which 22 EU members recognise. The EU should make visa relaxation with Serbia conditional on Serbia allowing Kosovo passport holders free transit through Serbia. Transit is not the same as recognition and would be a useful confidence building measure.

In an innovative development the British and Kosovan governments working with the British Council in Pristina announced in June 2011 a project aimed at improving "co-ordinated communication with Europe, including with non-recognising countries" and "a better understating of the benefits the dialogue with Serbia will bring to Kosovan people." One element of the new initiative was the "establishment of new channels of communication with non-recognising countries". Britain might reach out to other EU partners and jointly appoint special envoys to explain (in Latin America and other regions where the Kosovo story is not well known) why it makes sense to recognize the new nation. Similarly, they may encourage Moscow to stop its blocking tactics.

There are other measures that Europe can take which can help Kosovo. The most important is to get to know the country, its people and its politicians. The national parliaments of Europe should create friendship groups that can visit Kosovo and develop political contacts. Kosovan politicians might also ask themselves if they need to develop party political structures more closely aligned to those elsewhere in Europe instead of the clannish, highly personalized political structures. The winner-takes-all politics of Albania where the main object appears to be the crushing of any political opponent is a politics Kosovo should avoid. Political structures, political parties, political behaviour as well as politicians themselves cannot be imposed from outside a nation. Shaping a political class is never easy. Kosovo can also help by choosing as candidates men, and especially women, who can represent the nation with style and impact abroad.

Two striking beautiful young women now represent the new post-conflict generation of Kosovan politicians. Atifete Jahjaga was born in 1975 and studied law at Leicester University before working first as a lawyer and then as a police officer where she rose to be deputy head of the Kosovo police service. She was elected as president of Kosovo in 2011 and became the first female head of state of a Balkans nation where heavyset masculine patriarchal politics has long been the norm. She shares a small Pristina apartment with her husband, a dentist. Speaking clear English she sets out her plans to bring women's political networking events to Kosovo and be a spokesperson for a new generation of women politicians in the Balkans unencumbered by the hates of the past. Her colleague, Vlora Çitaku, was only 29 when she was named as Kosovo's Minister for European Integration in 2011. These two women and other younger politicians in Kosovo represent a 21st-century future. Balkans politics have been over-dominated by men for too long.

Russia's veto of Kosovo's place as a full member is, of course, cynical. In private, Russian policy-makers admit that if one of the Kremlin's foreign policy demands was met – the recognition of the Kremlin's annexation of Abkhazia, for example – Moscow would ditch Serbia overnight. Given Georgia's refusal to recognize Kosovo some might think the trade was a fair deal. There are many cynical diplomats but cynical diplomacy where every state has its price and no government has any values achieves little. Instead of looking for a zero-sum deal with Russia it would be better to work in other areas where Kosovo's status as a nation and a partial state can be acknowledged.

One institution is the Council of Europe where the majority of countries do recognize Kosovo. Council of Europe member states should make the case for Kosovo to have observer status and even if this proves difficult this should encourage regular visits by Kosovan delegations to its Parliamentary Assembly meetings. The Council of Europe took a lead in the 1990s by extending its membership to countries like Serbia even if Serbia's status was questioned by some. Membership of the Council of Europe implies recognition of the European Convention on Human Rights. Kosovans should have the right to the protection of the ECHR and to appeal to the European Court of Human Rights.

One proposal sometimes advanced is a partition of Kosovo. Daniel Hamilton, one of the British Conservative Party's young thoughtful international affairs experts, visits Kosovo regularly and argues that "A territorial division, at the Ibar, would end the ludicrous situation in which an international land border is enforced (at tremendous cost) between Serbia and Kosovo Serbs. Such a division would also be beneficial to Albanians, giving them full control over the country, as opposed to seeking to impose their will on a Serb population which has no interest in being part of their newly-independent state." In fact, the Serb population in Kosovo is more or less evenly divided between those who live in the region north of the Ibar and those who live elsewhere in Kosovo.

Partition has always seduced London-based foreign policy experts and was a demand raised regularly in the 1970s and 1980s by those who saw it as a magic solution to the problem of the Northern Irish conflict. But without unacceptable mass expulsions there is no partition that can finally settle the problem of a nation with different and conflicting communities living in it.

There is a possible exchange as the Preševo Valley region just to Kosovo's east has a majority Albanian population. Could a land-swap work? It should not be dismissed out of hand, although the main motorway linking the Alps to the Aegean runs through the Presevo Valley and it is hard to see Belgrade accepting Kosovan rule over its principal transport artery. Kosovo's foreign minister, Enver Hoxhaj, discussed the idea of partition with his Bulgarian counterpart on a visit to Sofia in June 2011. He made the important point that the creation of mono-ethnic nations runs counter to European values. Partition would be ethnic cleansing by the back door. "The issue of borders, states, and territories in the region is actually a closed chapter. We would never accept ideas of ethnic and territorial partitions because these ideas would create instability, they would produce violence, and the whole region would simply go back as it was 20 years ago. We are not at all in favor of creating monoethnic states in the region but we should have heterogeneous states and societies. In that sense, no one is supporting the idea partition," Hoxhaj explained

On the other hand Pristina should offer the maximum devolution to its troubled Serb-oriented northern region. Swiss cantons have tax, education, policing and other powers within an overall Swiss framework. In Alpine Italy the German-speaking south Tyrol which has always seen itself as part of Austria lives under the overall authority of the Italian state. Catalonia has its distinct national authority over its territory within the broader framework of Spain's devolved constitutional framework.

Certainly Pristina must do all in its power to stamp hard on Albanian militaristic nationalism. Ten years ago in his book *Kosovo: War and Revenge* Tim Judah argued, "We have severed the head of Greater Serbia only to discover that Balkan nationalism is hydra-headed". Judah expressed concern about "a rabid, expansionist Albanian nationalism, which [is aimed at creating] either a Greater Albania or at least a Greater Kosovo". These fears have proved to be unfounded. Tirana is careful to hose down any suggestions of a Greater Albania. There are tensions in Macedonia between the two communities but Albanian-speaking Macedonians do not call to join Albania or Kosovo. Arms caches left over from KLA days have been uncovered but Albanian-speaking Serb citizens in the Preševo Valley show no interest in any politics that would re-ignite political conflict or violence.

Partition therefore, while it has its superficial attractions, is never the real answer. That requires serious negotiation over the status of Serb areas in Kosovo between Belgrade and Pristina. Alternatively NATO and EULEX should exercise the authority of the UN and Europe and insist it is the international rule-of-law that prevails.

What happens now? The absence of creative, tolerant, win-win leadership in the Western Balkans in the second decade since the end of the wars is worrying. But how can Europe ask the region to embrace multiculturalism and an end of über-nationalism when President Sarkozy, Chancellor Merkel and Prime Minister Cameron denounce multiculturalism and insist on the primacy of their nation's self-interest over common European interest? As Ivan Krastev has written, "Serbia has lost Kosovo, but it still has not found itself." Europe's needs to refocus on the Western Balkans and help Serbia find its way, together with Kosovo as the British Foreign Secretary William Hague has urged, to a common EU future.

David Marquand in the plangent pessimism of his book, *The End of the West: The Once and Future Europe*, argues that

> In Europe we have to learn to live with one another; living with one another means accepting difference, rejoicing in

difference, and negotiating differences. That is the inner meaning of the Good Friday agreement to Northern Ireland, of asymmetric devolution in Spain, of the emergence of a federal Belgium, or the secession of Slovakia from what used to be Czechoslovakia… Slowly, sometimes reluctantly and even painfully, European peoples and countries are beginning to come to terms with difference, to accept its inevitability and legitimacy, and to bridge differences that once seemed unbridgeable.

Kosovo and Serbia must accept what has happened and move on. They have to write their future, no longer reliving their 20th-century history. Neither nation has a future if they believe and act as if they were still Balkans nations. They both should aspire to be European nations. That means a new Serbia and a new Kosovo. The sooner the better.

Bibliography

Berdal, Mats and Economides, Spyros (Editors). *United Nations Interventionism 1991–2004*, Cambridge: Cambridge University Press, 2007.

Bojičić – Dželilović, Vesna. "Transnational networks and state building in the Balkans", in *Open Democracy*, 17 January 2011.

Booth, Ken (Editor). *The Kosovo Tragedy: the Human Rights Dimensions*, London and Portland, Oregon: Frank Cass Publishers, 2001.

Chandler, David. *From Kosovo to Kabul and Beyond: Human Rights and International Intervention*, London: Pluto Press, 2006.

Davies, John. *'My Name is Not Natasha' How Albanian Women in France Use Trafficking to Overcome Social Exclusion (1998–2001)*, Amsterdam: Amsterdam University Press, 2009.

Di Lellio, Anna. *The Battle of Kosovo 1389: An Albanian Epic*, London and New York: I.B. Tauris, 2009.

——(Editor). *The Case for Kosovo: Passage to Independence*, London and New York: Anthem Press, 2006.

Durham, Mary Edith (Author) and Destani, Bejtullah (Editor). *Albania and the Albanians: Selected Articles and Letters 1903 – 1944*, London: The Centre for Albanian Studies, 2001.

Elsie, Robert. "Historical Dictionary of Kosovo", in *Historical Dictionaries of Europe*, No. 79, Plymouth, Toronto and Lanham: The Scarecrow Press, Inc., 2011.

European Commission. *Kosovo 2010 Progress Report*, COM(2010)660, 9 November 2010.

European Stability Initiative. *Isolation Confirmed: How the EU is undermining its interests in Kosovo*, 22 November 2010.

Glenny, Misha. *The Balkans 1804 – 1999: Nationalism, War and the Great Powers*, London: Granta Books, 1999.

——*McMafia: Seriously Organized Crime*, London: Vintage Books, 2009.

International Court of Justice Advisory Opinion on Kosovo's declaration of independence, Commons Library Standard Note SN/IA/5948, 4 May 2011.

International Crisis Group. *North Kosovo: Dual Sovereignty in Practice*, Europe Report no. 211, 14 March 2011.

——*Kosovo and Serbia after the ICJ opinion*, Europe report no. 206, 26 August 2010.

Judt, Tony. *Postwar: A History of Europe since 1945*, London: William Heinemann, 2005.

Kouchner, Bernard. *Les Guerriers de la Paix*, Paris: Grasset & Fasquelle, 2004.

Malcolm, Noel. *Kosovo: A Short History*, London and Basingstoke: Macmillan, 1998.

Marinković, Milan. "Serbia and Kosovo: a war of nerves", in *Open Democracy*, 22 April 2011.

Parliamentary Assembly of the Council of Europe, Committee on Legal Affairs and Human Rights. *Inhuman treatment of people and illicit trafficking in human organs in Kosovo: Report*. Rapporteur: Dick Marty, Switzerland, Alliance of Liberals and Democrats for Europe), 12 December 2010.

Recognition of Kosovo, Commons Library Standard Note SN/IA/4690, 9 April 2008.

Schwartz, Stephen. *Kosovo: Background to a War*, London: Anthem Press, 2000.

Sebastian, Sofía. *Spanish Foreign Policy in the Balkans: Wasted Potential*, Policy Brief no. 28, FRIDE, January 2010.

———*Making Kosovo Work*, Policy Brief no. 7, FRIDE, March 2009.

Sewell, John. *The Balkan Economics: Regional Roadblocks, European Distractions and Global Crisis*, Sub-Committee on East-West Economic Cooperation and Convergence, NATO Parliamentary Assembly, 084 ESCEW 11 E, 14th March 2011.

Simms, Brendan. *Unfinest Hour: Britain and the Destruction of Bosnia*, London: Penguin Press, 1991.

von Sydow, Björn. *Situation in Kosovo*, Political Affairs Committee, European Parliamentary Assembly, 11 March 2010. Accessed on 28/06/2011 http://www.assembly.coe.int/CommitteeDocs/2010/Sydow_Kosovo_E.pdf

Wählisch, Martin. "Three years after independence, Kosovo still struggles for recognition", in *Open Democracy*, 17 February 2011.

Weymouth, Tony and Henig, Stanley (Editors). *The Kosovo Crisis: The last American war in Europe?*, Edinburgh and London: Reuters, Pearson Education Limited, 2001.